THE AMERICAN SAILING ASSOCIATION'S

LET'S GO SAILING

**OFFICIAL MANUAL FOR THE AMERICAN SAILING ASSOCIATION'S
BASIC SMALL BOAT STANDARD (ASA110)**

by

PETER ISLER

Produced for ASA by

Amanda Lunn Design and Publishing

www.amandalunnpublishing.com

proofreader Jo Weeks

indexer Penelope Kent

illustrator Peter Bull

ASA

editor Cindy Shabes

technical editor Marly Isler

publisher Lenny Shabes

First published by American Sailing Association in 2019

American Sailing Association
5301 Beethoven Street, Suite #265
Los Angeles, CA 90066

ISBN 978-1-7331628-0-7

Printed in the U.S.

www.asa.com

CONTENTS

INTRODUCTION

Welcome to the world of sailing. In this book, we introduce small boat sailing – following the American Sailing Association's ASA110 – Basic Small Boat Sailing Standard. Learning to sail in a small boat is the best way to start – since its size and light weight provide the new sailor with immediate feedback to adjustments of sail trim, weight position and steering. We strongly recommend that you start out by taking lessons from an experienced sailor. Around the world are hundreds of ASA certification facilities with experienced and accredited instructors that can get you started in this great sport. A sailboat can take you across the lake or around the globe – it's an activity that you can enjoy for the rest of your life – with many fascinating and fun aspects to explore. Welcome aboard – let's go sailing!

There are many types of boats that fall into the general category of "small boat", from catamarans to centerboard dinghies – even small keelboats. For the purposes of this book we will focus on two "generic" types – the twin-hulled catamaran and the single hulled dinghy. Although different in appearance – they are so similar in the way that they sail that one can learn the basic skills of small boat sailing in either type. So, most of the lessons and material in this book apply equally to both catamarans and dinghies. Where there are important differences – we will make note. There is a glossary on page 90 to help you learn sailing terminology. And thoughout the book glossary words are italicized.

Dinghy – A sailboat with a single hull which has a centerboard, daggerboard, or leeboard (never a fixed keel – which is only found on a keelboat) and usually, one rudder. Dinghies range in size from small singlehanded craft with a single sail to boats 20 feet or longer that can carry a crew of three (or more) and can fly up to three sails.

Catamaran – A two hulled boat – with two rudders. Some small cats have additional underwater foils such as a centerboard or daggerboard – but many do not. Like the monohull dinghy, cats range from small, singlehanded craft with a single sail up to 20 feet or longer that can carry a larger crew and more sails.

Peter Isler
TWO-TIME AMERICA'S CUP-WINNING NAVIGATOR

Safety first — Sailing in small boats is fun, partly because you are so close to the water that you get wet. And most learn-to-sail courses in small boats start out getting the students real wet with a "swim test", or more accurately, a "float test" – with life jacket and sailing clothes. And that makes good sense, since capsizing is very much a part of small boat sailing. And being comfortable moving around in the water to be able to right your boat and get sailing again is a basic skill every sailor must learn. No matter how good of a swimmer you are, a life jacket should always be worn when sailing small boats. In chapter three we cover capsizing and other safety subjects as well as what to wear so you are comfortable on the water. Make sure you read that chapter before your first sail.

CHAPTER 1
Beginning to sail

THE WIND AND THE SAILOR

If you have ever spent any time on or near the water, you have experienced an exciting and ever changing world. Winds can whip up the water's surface into foamy waves in no time. Lack of wind can leave the surface as smooth as glass. Out on the water sailing, your interest in wind and weather grows.

FEEL THE WIND

Because your boat is so dependent on the wind, your ability to "feel" the wind – to assess its direction and speed and how those can change is essential. In fact, the first step in learning to sail should be to hone those skills and increase your sensitivity and awareness of it. The best way to track the wind is simply to feel it. Your body, especially your face, can feel the exact direction of the wind if you concentrate. Practice this whenever you can.

Visual aids also help to determine the wind direction. A sailor is always watching for those clues such as a fluttering flag or the sail trim of a passing sailboat. By studying the water you can often see waves or maybe tiny ripples. This water motion is caused by the wind. And ripples and waves often get pushed into lines that are 90 degrees to the wind's direction. Once you gain more experience, you will be able to judge the wind speed by looking at the water. For example, in open water, *whitecaps* – waves with a foamy white top – begin to form in wind speeds of about 12 knots.

....

TIP *Sailors and weather forecasters often use nautical miles rather than land-based statute miles to measure distance and speed (knots). A knot is 15 percent faster than a mile per hour.*

....

The wind is the center of a sailor's universe. Use every sense to find, and pay attention to its direction and speed.

Ripples and waves   Direction and sail trim of sailboats

Flapping sails

See and feel
the wind

Flags

Other visual signs of the wind are boats. A sailboat under sail is a great indicator that you will learn to use as you become a sailor. Clues will include a sailboat's direction, its sail trim, and the position of the sailors on board. Anchored boats will point toward the wind unless there is a strong *current*. A wind vane, flag, or a short length of yarn attached to the rigging on your boat can show the wind, and so can a flapping sail – which will wave "downwind" like a flag.

REMEMBER A sailor's world revolves around

Wind vanes

WIND

Leaves blowing

Direction of boats at anchor

THE WIND A sailor is always trying to "see" the wind and watching for clues to determine the wind's strength and direction.

the wind and assessing and staying aware of the wind's direction is crucial. When you are just beginning to sail – you may feel so inundated with all of the new information that it's easy to lose track of the wind direction. If that happens, just relax, take a deep breath and feel the wind on your face and skin. Your ability to accurately sense changes in the wind, its speed and its direction will improve as you learn. This is an important transition that will occur as you become a sailor.

SAILORS' LANGUAGE

Your next step is to feel comfortable and at home on your sailboat. As you probably know from reading books and watching movies, sailing has its own language-terminology. It will take some time before you are comfortable with all of these new terms. Don't force it or get frustrated learning every name for every little piece on the boat right away. You want to sail the boat, not talk about it. With time and practice you will assimilate this new language and it will become your own.

SAILBOAT PARTS AND TERMINOLOGY

Here are common words that you will come across on your first sail. They will become old friends soon enough – you don't have to memorize them all at once. Every sailboat is slightly different in the way it is designed and rigged. Although most of these terms are common to all boats, you will find differences. For example, a catamaran has two *hulls* and a dinghy has one *hull* but they both use the wind in the same way. Many catamarans do not have a *boom*. But fundamentally – every sailboat is a sailboat.

The next few pages will introduce you to some parts and terms on several different boats. For more important sailing words – check out the glossary on page 90.

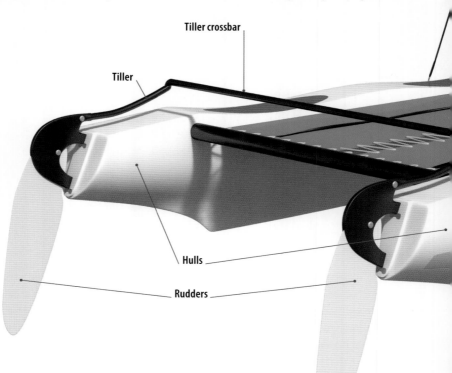

Tiller crossbar

Tiller

Hulls

Rudders

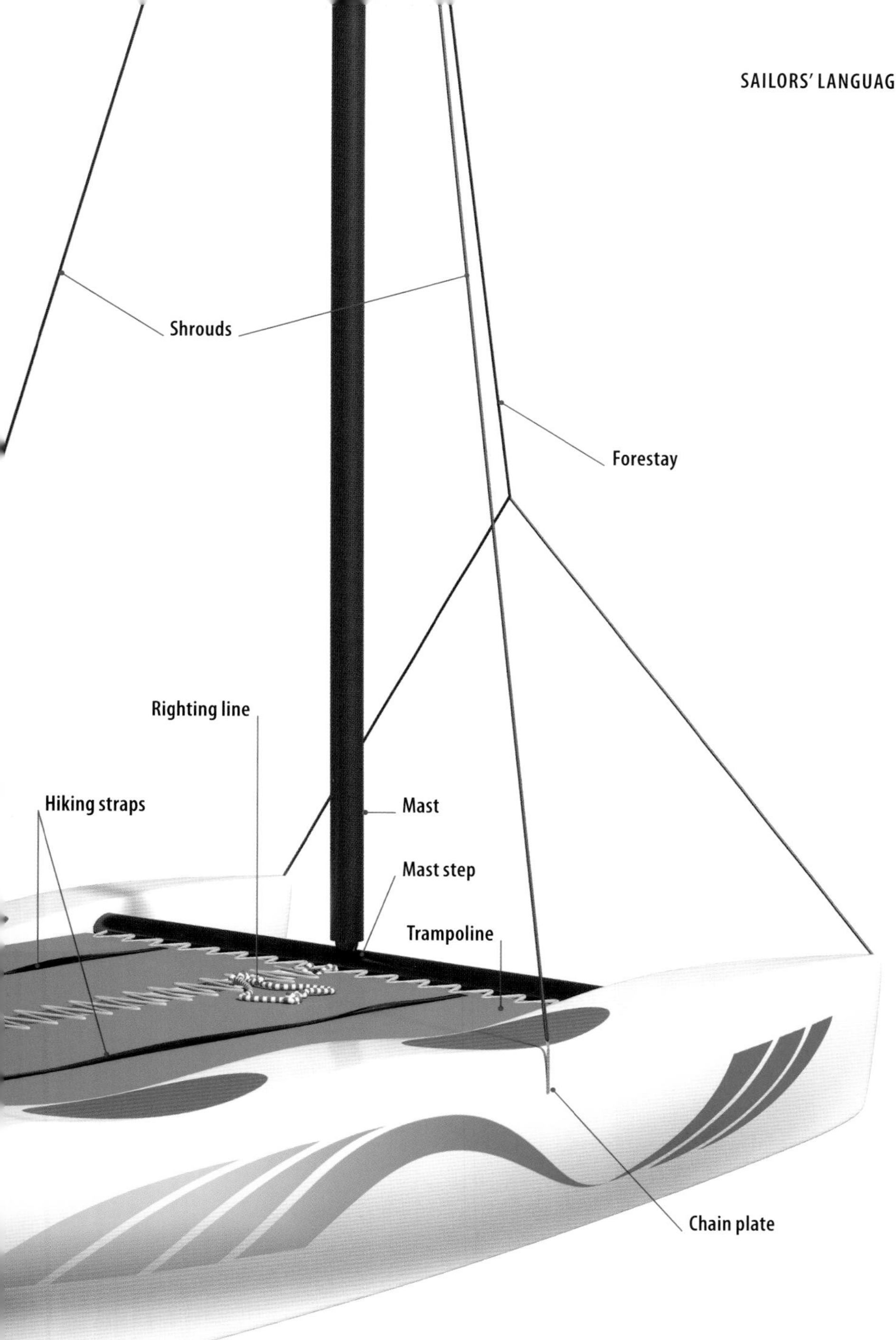

Shrouds

Forestay

Righting line

Hiking straps

Mast

Mast step

Trampoline

Chain plate

CATAMARAN A catamaran shares most features and parts with
its single-hulled brethren. But there are some parts that are
unique to these two-hulled sailboats.

It will take you some time to master this terminology. But as you spend time on the boat these words will become familiar. So, let's leave these terms to review later and get on to what you are really here for: sailing! If you forget a word or name while sailing, don't worry, it's more important to understand the big picture – the function of each part of the boat and how everything works together.

REMEMBER *Line* is the sailor's term for any rope on a boat and "running rigging" is all the parts used to hoist and trim the sails including *sheets*, *blocks*, *halyards*, *lines*, etc.

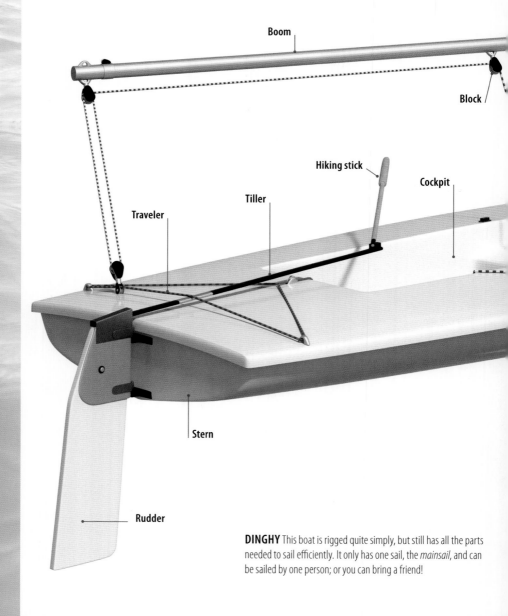

Boom

Block

Hiking stick

Cockpit

Tiller

Traveler

Stern

Rudder

DINGHY This boat is rigged quite simply, but still has all the parts needed to sail efficiently. It only has one sail, the *mainsail*, and can be sailed by one person; or you can bring a friend!

Mast

Gooseneck

Boom vang

Bow

Mainsheet

Cleat

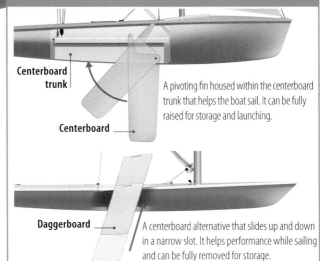

CENTERBOARD VS DAGGERBOARD

Centerboard
trunk

A pivoting fin housed within the centerboard trunk that helps the boat sail. It can be fully raised for storage and launching.

Centerboard

Daggerboard

A centerboard alternative that slides up and down in a narrow slot. It helps performance while sailing and can be fully removed for storage.

Daggerboard

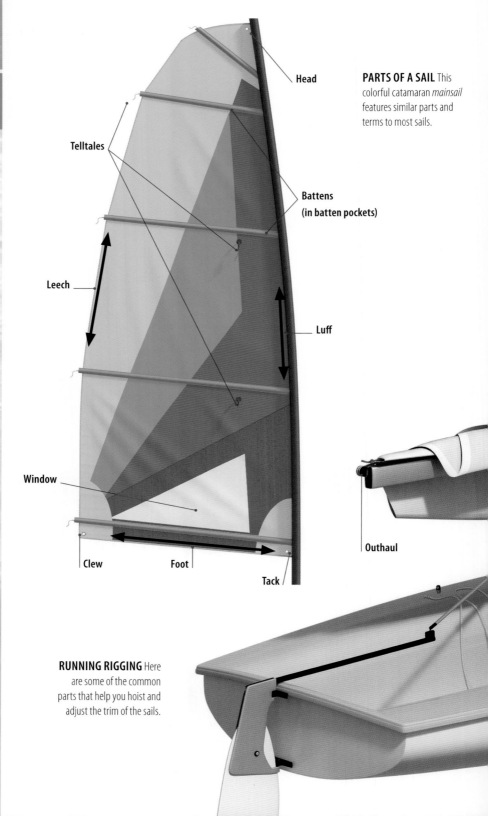

Head

PARTS OF A SAIL This colorful catamaran *mainsail* features similar parts and terms to most sails.

Telltales

Battens
(in batten pockets)

Leech

Luff

Window

Outhaul

Clew

Foot

Tack

RUNNING RIGGING Here are some of the common parts that help you hoist and adjust the trim of the sails.

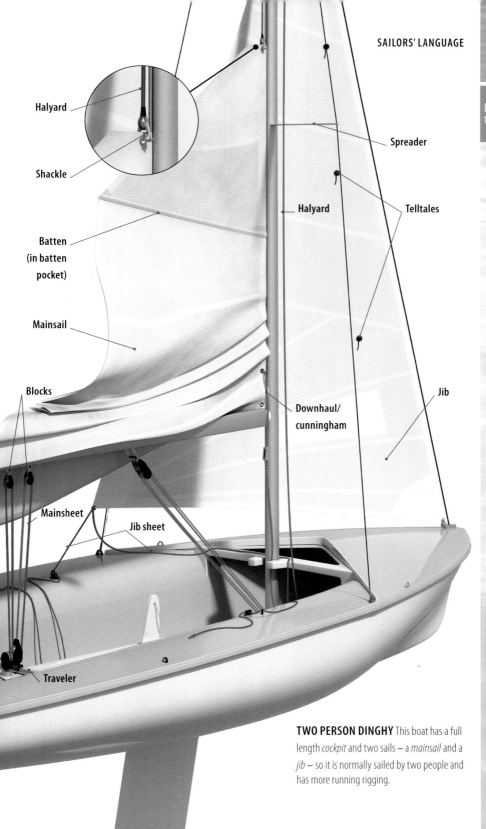

Halyard

Shackle

Batten
(in batten
pocket)

Mainsail

Blocks

Mainsheet

Jib sheet

Traveler

Spreader

Halyard

Telltales

Downhaul/
cunningham

Jib

TWO PERSON DINGHY This boat has a full
length *cockpit* and two sails – a *mainsail* and a
jib – so it is normally sailed by two people and
has more running rigging.

POINTS OF SAIL

Let's focus on your new-found awareness of the wind direction to learn more about sailing. No sailboat can sail directly "toward" the wind – it is physically impossible because the sail will not "fill." But by harnessing the forces created by air and water flow, a sailboat can sail remarkably "close" to the wind.

WIND DIRECTION

The points of sail are a super-important concept for any sailor to understand. They are the directions a boat can (and cannot sail) – relative to the wind direction – broken down into sectors. They relate to everything you do on the boat – from where you sit, to how fast you can go, and how the sails are best trimmed. It's important to be able to visualize the points of sail so let's draw a circle with the wind

direction coming from the top of the circle – at 12 o'clock. Now you can draw the sectors that are known as the points of sail.

On paper the points of sail are easy to see. The challenge is to apply this diagram and concept to the real world on the boat. This is when your ability to feel the wind will be very valuable. As you learn to sail, the *no sail zone* (and avoiding it) will be a key

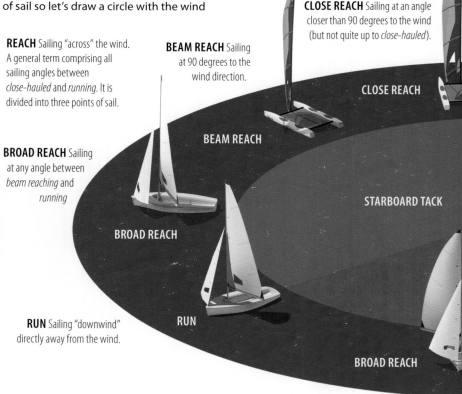

CLOSE REACH Sailing at an angle closer than 90 degrees to the wind (but not quite up to *close-hauled*).

CLOSE REACH

REACH Sailing "across" the wind. A general term comprising all sailing angles between *close-hauled* and *running*. It is divided into three points of sail.

BEAM REACH Sailing at 90 degrees to the wind direction.

BEAM REACH

BROAD REACH Sailing at any angle between *beam reaching* and *running*

STARBOARD TACK

BROAD REACH

RUN Sailing "downwind" directly away from the wind.

RUN

BROAD REACH

concept to translate into practice on the boat. Traveling in any other direction is possible and really quite easy.

REMEMBER You already know the wind direction is the center of your universe, so if you get confused, just find the wind direction and compare it to the boat's course.

PORT AND STARBOARD

■ **Port:** sailing word for left. The port side of the boat is its left side (facing toward the *bow*).
■ **Starboard:** sailing word for right. The starboard side of the boat is its right side.

A good way to remember is that the word "left" has fewer letters than "right" and so does its nautical cousin "port" compared to "starboard."

However, there is one time when the nautical words for right and left are important to use. (And once again it relates to the wind direction!) It is when you are describing which side of the points of sail diagram you are sailing on – upon which side of the boat the wind is blowing.

As you can see from the points of sail diagram, a *beam reach* can be sailed with the wind hitting either the right or the left side. To differentiate you introduce the terms *starboard tack* and *port tack*. There are a couple of tricks to determining which *tack* your boat is on. The first is, you guessed it, by simply feeling the wind direction. If it is coming over the left side, your boat is sailing along the *port tack* and vice versa. Another way is to look at the way the sails are set. If the wind is blowing the *mainsail* and *boom* out over the right side of the boat, then you are sailing on *port tack*. *Starboard tack* has the opposite features.

CLOSE-HAULED Sailing upwind as close to the wind as possible, also called *beating*. This point of sail is very narrow – just a few degrees.

NO SAIL ZONE The sector bisected by the wind direction where a sailboat cannot sail. It is about 90 degrees wide.

CLOSE-HAULED

WIND

IN IRONS

NO SAIL ZONE

PORT TACK

CLOSE-HAULED

CLOSE REACH

BEAM REACH

SAILS AND SAILING

Sails are your boat's engine and it doesn't matter how many sails your boat is flying, they all work the same way. Understanding how they work will help your sail trim skills.

HOW SAILS WORK

Sails harness the power of the wind and there are two ways a sail works to provide this power:

■ **Lift Mode:** The sail is operating like a wing (with the wind flowing across it on both sides).

■ **Drag Mode:** The sail is operating like a parachute ("blocking" the wind).

When sailing *close-hauled*, *close reaching* and *beam reaching*, the sails are working in lift mode. The wind is flowing "across" both sides of the sail's wind shape creating a force called lift. You have probably experienced this lifting force when you held your hand out of a moving car window. This force, combined with the force of the water flowing across the boat's underbody – the *hull*, *centerboard,* and *rudder*, drives the boat *forward* and, if it's windy enough causes the boat to lean sideways or *heel*.

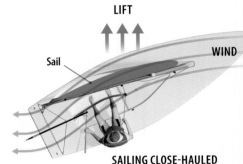

SAILING CLOSE-HAULED

Airplane wing

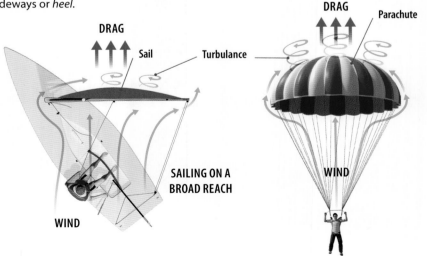

SAILING ON A BROAD REACH

On a *broad reach* or a *run* there is very little flow across the sails which are now acting more like a parachute – pulling the boat forward. This is drag mode.

POINTS OF SAIL AND TRIM

When you get on a boat for a sail, you will learn more about sail trim (how far you pull in or ease out a sail) to optimize its power. But while looking at the *points of sail* diagram it's worth visualizing the trim of the sail(s) (relative to the boat's *centerline*) on each point of sail. As you can see, the sails are pulled in closest to the boat's *centerline* when sailing *close-hauled*. As you move downwind from *close-hauled*, the optimum sail trim changes with the sails being "eased out" more and more until they are about 90 degrees to the boat's *centerline* when sailing on a *run*.

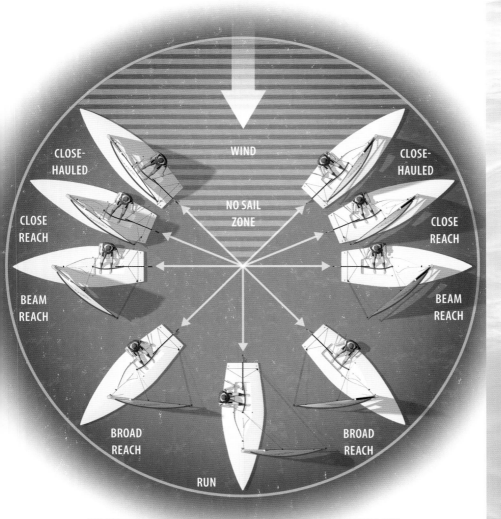

NOTICE HOW THE SAIL TRIM SHOULD CHANGE ON EVERY POINT OF SAIL

CHANGING YOUR POINT OF SAIL

When you move from one point of sail to the other, you must turn the boat. First, let's look at the smaller, simple turns where you stay on the same *tack* starting from a *beam reach*.

■ **Heading Up:** Any turn of the boat toward the wind. On a *beam reach* if you turn a few degrees toward the wind you will be on the *close reaching point of sail* – a rather wide zone. If you *head up* farther you will reach the *close-hauled* point of sail (or even the dreaded *no sail zone*). To keep optimal sail trim when you *head up*, you will trim in the sails.

■ **Heading Down** (*Bearing away*): Any turn of the boat away from the wind. As you *head down* from a *beam reach* you ease the sails to maintain optimum trim and you may have to slide your body "inboard" toward the *centerline* as the power of the sails decreases on the new "lower" point of sail.

....

TIP *Turning the* rudder *with the* tiller/tiller crossbar *is the easiest way to change direction when the boat is moving. But by moving your body laterally (inboard or outboard) even just a few inches you will have an effect on the boat's steering, its speed, and how much it* heels.

....

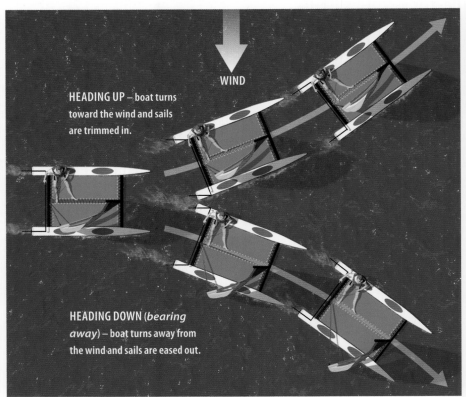

HEADING UP – boat turns toward the wind and sails are trimmed in.

WIND

HEADING DOWN (*bearing away*) – boat turns away from the wind and sails are eased out.

Every time you turn the boat – your point of sail changes so the sail trim should be adjusted. Practice *heading up* and *heading down* as shown, starting from a *beam reach*. Try turning with small *rudder* movements, and experiment with moving your body to help the turn. Lean inboard to *head up*, lean outboard to *head down*.

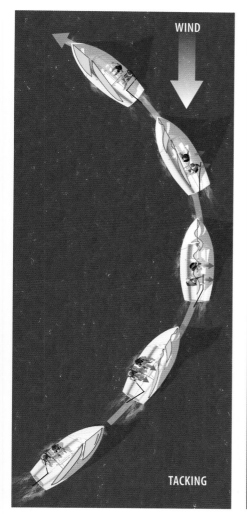

TACKING

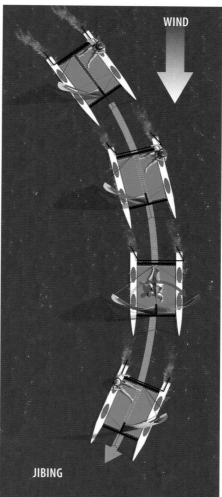

JIBING

CHANGING TACKS

When you turn so far that the boat moves from one side of the *points of sail* diagram to the other, you are "changing *tacks*" from *port tack* to *starboard tack* or vice versa. But you have a choice, there are two routes to get to the other *tack*, you can either *tack* or *jibe*. Warning – this can be confusing because the word *tack* has three meanings on a boat – luckily, you've already learned the other two: (a) front corner of the sail

and, (b) describing on what "side" of the *points of sail* you are sailing. Any time you change *tacks* the sails will feel the wind coming on their "other" side and be blown to the opposite side of the boat.

■ **Tacking:** Changing *tacks* by *heading up* and turning all the way through the *no sail zone* to the other side.

■ **Jibing:** Changing *tacks* by *heading down* to a *run* and continuing the turn until the sails come across and fill on the opposite side.

THE NO SAIL ZONE

When first learning to sail, it is very common to lose speed until you have no maneuverability. Just like a car or bicycle, if your boat isn't moving, then steering will have no effect. When the boat loses all speed while pointing in the *no sail zone* you are officially stuck *in irons*! Some boats are more prone to this ignominy than others, especially catamarans, which lose maneuverability at low speed due to the drag of the two *hulls*. It's important to understand that it's perfectly okay for a sailboat to be in the *no sail zone* temporarily. Every time a boat *tacks* it passes through the *no sail zone*. It's only when you lose speed while in the zone that you risk losing your steering control.

IN IRONS The condition where the boat has lost forward motion while pointing in the *no sail zone*.

RUNNING AND SAILING BY THE LEE

180 degrees from the *no sail zone* is the point of sail called a *run*. Normally sailors avoid this point of sail, especially in strong winds, because it requires hyper attention to the wind direction to avoid sailing *by the lee* and risking an accidental (unintentional) *jibe* – a potentially dangerous situation when the *boom* comes flying across the centerline unexpectedly.

Next, you will get to the fun part by rigging your boat and going for a sail. Just remember to keep the learning process in perspective. Don't get bogged down with the terminology. Simply find that wind direction and stay attuned to it. The rest will come with time.

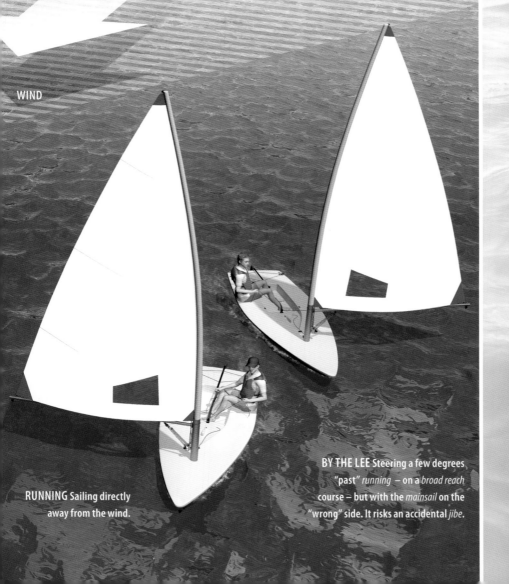

WIND

RUNNING Sailing directly
away from the wind.

BY THE LEE Steering a few degrees
"past" *running* – on a *broad reach*
course – but with the *mainsail* on the
"wrong" side. It risks an accidental *jibe*.

REVIEW QUESTIONS (see page 96 for answers)

CHOOSE FROM THE ANSWERS PROVIDED

1 What is the single most important concept for a new sailor to understand?

a Sailboats work like airplanes

b A centerboard boat is the best boat on which to learn

c The terms port and starboard

d The relationship between the boat and the wind

e Sailing is different on square riggers

2 Which of the following signs help a sailor to determine the wind direction? (Choose all that apply)

a The direction of the ripples on the water

b The direction of the current

c The direction and sail trim of other sailboats underway

d The direction an anchored boat points

e The feel of the wind on your cheek

3 Why is it important to distinguish between port and starboard tack? (Choose the best answer)

a Because it helps you to understand the points of sail and the concept of changing tacks (tacking or jibing)

b Because sailboats cannot sail directly upwind

c Because port is left and starboard is right on a sailboat

d Because the sailor must be able to feel the wind

e Because you want to stay out of irons

4 Which of the following are NOT true? (Choose all that are not true)

a Port is left on a sailboat

b If the boom is being blown off the right side of the hull, you are on starboard tack

c Starboard is right on a sailboat

d One can sail a beam reach on either port or starboard tack

e The no sail zone only happens on starboard tack

5 What is the difference between tacking and jibing? (Choose the best answer)

a One is done on port tack and the other on starboard tack

b One can only be done in strong winds

c One can be done without changing tacks

d One is changing tacks by turning toward the wind and the other is changing tacks by turning away from the wind

e Tacking can be done only on centerboard boats

6 Which of the following is NOT true about tacking and jibing?

a One is done on port tack and the other is done on starboard tack

b Right before a jibe the sails are working in "drag" mode

c After a tack or jibe, the boat has changed tacks

d One is changing tacks by turning toward the wind and the other is changing tacks by turning away from the wind

e Sailing by the lee can happen when jibing

7 How can you avoid being stuck in irons? (Choose the best answer)

a Use only correct terminology when sailing

b Always keep the boat moving so you have steering control

c Duck your head when you jibe to avoid being hit with the boom

d Hoist your main halyard very high

e Don't sail in tidal waters

8 The points of sail and general principles of sailing are different on a catamaran than on a monohull. ("True" or "False")

9 Why can sailing by the lee be dangerous? (Choose the best answer)

a Because the mainsail is eased out all the way

b Because the centerboard is raised up

c Because you have to steer with your body weight

d Because of the risk of an accidental jibe

e Because you can't feel the wind as well

2

CHAPTER 2
Let's go sailing

RIGGING THE BOAT

There are so many types of boats, each with its own rigging variations, but the basics of getting ready to sail remain the same. Your instructor will be the best source of information with any rigging questions. It is also helpful to watch other people getting ready to sail. Let's look at the common features and steps of rigging and launching a small sailboat.

PLAN AHEAD

First, make sure you have all of the gear and equipment that you and your boat need to go sailing. You may laugh, but many great sailing adventures have been thwarted because of a forgotten item. It may help to have a checklist to ensure that your trip to the water is not wasted.

REMEMBER This is a rule for the rest of your sailing career: The easier it is to get the boat sailing, the more sailing you will do.

RIG THE MAST

Even in the best-case scenario – where your boat is sitting *mast* up on the smooth beach a few feet from the water in a protected area with no waves – you will have some rigging work to do.

....
TIP *It is invaluable to have an instructor/sailor experienced in the layout and rigging of the particular boat to help guide you through the steps of rigging the first time.*
....

Turn the rigging process into a routine so that you can do it easily and quickly. An initial step may be setting up the *mast* (if it is not already up). If the *mast* is heavy, an extra hand can make the lifting process easier. Once the *mast* has been set into its *mast step*, make sure any and all supporting wires (*shrouds* and *forestay*) are securely fixed into position. Take an extra minute to inspect the fittings where they attach to ensure nothing is loose or in danger of failing. A dismasting due to a rigging error, though uncommon, can ruin a good day.

With both *shrouds* attached, and the *mast* secured to the *mast step*, this *mast* can be easily raised by pulling on a rope tied to extend the *forestay*

ATTACH THE SAILS

Once the *mast* is up, the sails can be rigged on many, but not all boats. Some small boats have a *mainsail* with a sleeve along the front edge. On these boats you must first slide the sail sleeve onto the *mast* at ground level and then put the *mast* and sail up together. But if your boat's sails must be "hoisted" up an already standing *mast* – then the following general steps often apply.

If your boat has one – fix the *boom* to the *mast* (at the *gooseneck*). The *mainsail* is then fixed onto the *boom* with both bottom corners attached securely and tensioned. Next, make sure the *battens* are in place and properly secured. It's easy to forget to put the *battens* in a sail – and if they are not secured they can slip out when the hoisted sail flaps. Without *battens* secure in their "pockets" the sail will stretch and flap constantly.

ATTACHING A MAINSAIL WITH A SLEEVE

On many boats – especially larger ones – the sails are hoisted by a *halyard*.

The *halyard's* attachment is normally made with a *shackle* or by tying a secure knot like a *bowline* to the sail's *head*. Check that the *mainsail* is not twisted around the *boom* and that the *halyard* runs clear from the sail to the top of the *mast*. Also make

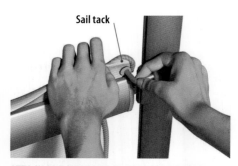

ATTACH THE MAINSAIL TACK TO ITS FITTING

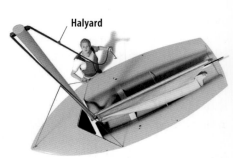

CHECK THAT THE HALYARD IS FREE TO RUN

CHECK THAT THE BATTENS ARE SECURELY INSERTED

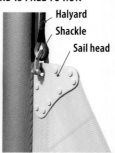

ATTACH THE MAINSAIL HEAD TO THE HALYARD

sure the *mainsheet* is rigged properly to the *boom* (or the *clew* of the sail as is common on many catamarans) with no twists and is not cleated and is free to run.

If your boat has a *jib* – it must be rigged by attaching the sail's *tack* to a fitting on or near the *bow*. The *jib sheets* should be attached to the back corner (*clew*) and rigged through the proper *blocks*, *fairleads*, and/or *cleats*. Again, ensure that any *battens* are in place and secure the *jib halyard* to the sail's *head*. By pulling the *halyard* taut and away from the *mast* you can easily see any wraps or tangles which should be unwound before attaching it to the sail and hoisting.

The timing of when you hoist the sail will depend on the specific launching situation. As a general rule – don't raise your sails until you and the boat are ready to go sailing. That means being in position to either immediately launch the boat – or push off from the dock or beach. A sudden wind shift or gust can cause the hoisted sails to fill and make the boat difficult to control if you are not prepared. Always ensure that the *sheets* of any hoisted sail are uncleated and free to run out until you are in the boat and ready to sail.

FINAL PREPARATION BEFORE LAUNCHING

Now check and drain all watertight compartments taking special care to secure the plugs, covers or flaps that prevent water from entering the boat and its compartments. You are now almost ready to launch the boat into the water. It's time to make sure that you have all the boat's equipment aboard (e.g. *rudder*, *tiller*, *daggerboard*, *bailer*) and any other personal gear you want to bring. Ensure that any

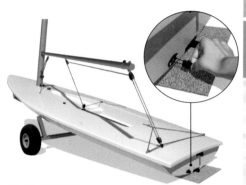

CHECK FOR WATER IN THE HULL AND DRAIN

loose gear is securely stowed so that you won't lose it overboard.

It is now time to put on any sailing clothing (foul weather gear, gloves, lifejacket) before getting the boat into the water.

....

TIP *On many small boats there is not much storage space, so limit what you bring to the essentials. If you want to bring your cell phone, make sure it is in a floating waterproof holder that can be secured to you or the boat.*

....

CHECK YOUR SURROUNDINGS

Take a look around to identify any power wires that could touch your *mast* while moving the boat to the water. Remember: power wires might go over the water too.

LAUNCHING THE BOAT

The wind direction continues to play an important role as you get your boat into the water (launch) and ready to sail. By paying attention to the wind and waves you can make your life a lot easier when launching.

GETTING INTO THE WATER

Although boats are well constructed to handle the stresses of sailing they must be handled carefully on shore. You will be using either a trailer (or smaller "dolly") or manpower to get the boat to the water.

Always try to enlist more than enough people if the boat must be carried. It makes it easier and safer for all involved. Once the boat is afloat you must choose a safe spot where you will hoist the sails.

BOW TOWARD THE WIND

Sometimes your launching situation (or your boat type) will allow you to hoist your *mainsail* before launching. But in many cases it may be better to wait until the boat is floating to hoist. This is because the wind blowing on the sails can make it difficult to handle the boat as you launch it.

Your goal is to find a location where the boat can be held (or tied) with the *bow* pointing toward the wind while the *rudder*(s)

A DOLLY FACILITATES BEACH LAUNCHING

and *centerboard* (if any) are put in place and the sails are hoisted. If there is a nearby dock or buoy on which to tie up then use it. If not, enlist the services of your crew or a helpful onlooker to wade into the water and hold the *bow* of your boat while the sails are hoisted.

BEACH/RAMP LAUNCHING

If you are launching off the beach never leave the boat half in and half out of the water. Any wave action will hurt the *hull* by grinding it on the rocks or sand or even push the boat out into the water. If there are any waves, take great care and keep the boat pointed perpendicular to the waves so they cannot push on the *hull* so hard.

DOCK/BUOY LAUNCHING

Launching off a dock is easier than a ramp or beach, especially if the dock's edge is

THINK OF YOUR SAFETY

Even if you are an Olympic swimmer you should always wear a *life jacket* when sailing small boats. It should become a habit — like wearing a seat belt in a car. Make sure your *life jacket* is comfortable so that it's easy to wear — always!

well padded so that you can simply slide the boat into the water.

Once in the water move the boat to the side of the dock that enables the *bow* to point toward the wind. Avoid the side of the dock upon which the wind blows (*windward* side) when launching and docking. This is an important concept to understand. The direction of the wind is critical even when choosing a good spot from which to depart or return.

WIND

FINAL RIGGING

Now that your boat is in the water it is time to climb aboard and hoist the sails. If your boat is tied to a dock or buoy make sure that it is tied securely with a good knot. (See page 84 for some great knots). If your boat was beach launched and is being held by someone standing in the water – ensure it is pointing toward the wind by holding at the *bow* or from the side at the *shroud* – no farther than 1/3 of the way back from the *bow*.

If you have ever stepped into a canoe or rowboat you will know how tippy they can be. With its two *hulls* a catamaran is very stable without sails hoisted – but a dinghy can be pretty tippy so step into the boat carefully – using your hands for support and trying to keep your weight low and near the *centerline*. Once in the boat, slide the *centerboard* (if any) down all the way. If you are launching off a beach it may be too shallow so simply put it down as far as you can safely. This underwater fin will steady the boat and make it easier for you to move around and complete the rigging process.

A catamaran will likely have its *rudders* and *tiller* already attached and flipped up out of the water. Now is the time to put them down into the water. On a monohull dinghy the *rudder* attaches to the back of the boat. (Ensure there is a safety clip or rope so the *rudder* will stay with the boat if you *capsize*). If separate – attach the *tiller* securely to the *rudder*. You are now ready to hoist the sail(s).

On a boat with two sails, a *mainsail* and a *jib*, it's really your choice as to which sail to hoist first. You may find it easiest to put up the *mainsail* last so that the swinging *boom* won't hamper your movement in the boat. When hoisting a *mainsail* – the top corner (*head*) is usually inserted into a slot on the back side of the *mast* before hoisting. Often

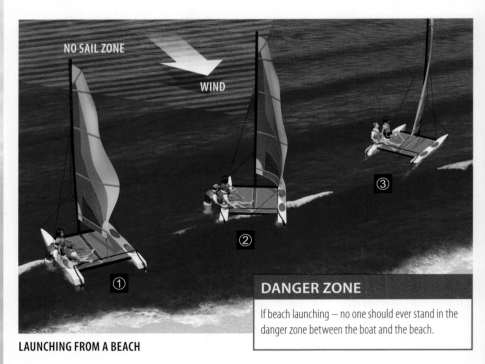

LAUNCHING FROM A BEACH

NO SAIL ZONE

WIND

① ② ③

DANGER ZONE

If beach launching — no one should ever stand in the danger zone between the boat and the beach.

the sail will have a *bolt rope* along the front edge (*luff*) that will have to be fed into the *mast* slot during hoisting. The *halyard*(s) should be pulled up tightly and cleated securely. Once the sails are up your crew should get aboard. You want to start sailing soon to avoid excessive flapping of the sails (and an accidental "bonk" on the head from the shaking *boom* or *mainsail*). If you do have to stay tied up for a short while make sure the sails' control ropes (*sheets*) are free to run so the sails will not fill and push the boat around.

SAILING AWAY

You should already have been paying attention to the wind direction and been considering the best course to take to get out into open water. And since the boat is pointing toward the wind – you are currently in the *no sail zone* where the sails don't power the boat – they only flap. No

matter from where you are starting out, you will make your departure easier by getting some *forward* momentum so that the *rudder* will be able to start working and you can steer out of the *no sail zone*. You may have to get creative to get moving – a push from a friend or by pulling the dock *line* – even running along in shallow water and then jumping on board.

GETTING UNDERWAY

① Boat pointed toward the wind, check that the crew and the boat are prepared for sailing, sails fully *luffing*.
② Sails still fully *luffing*, get forward motion (pushing boat or pulling *bow line*) and rotate the boat out of the *no sail zone* by turning the *rudder*.
③ Once rotated out of the *no sail zone* slowly trim sails, steer straight and sail off on a *close reach*.

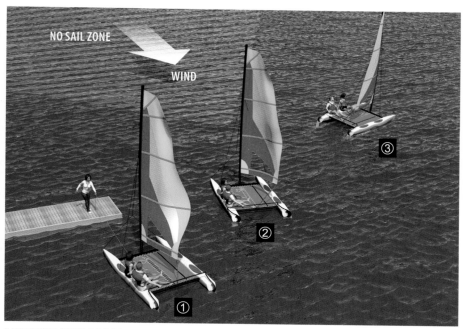

LAUNCHING FROM A DOCK

YOUR FIRST SAIL

Once under sail, you will be set free with the wind. It is a great feeling to cast off all ties with the shore. Hopefully you have a good day to start out with nice "medium" (5–12 knots) winds – not too light and not too strong. That's the ideal for your first few sails.

PICK THE RIGHT WIND

If the wind is so light that there are barely any ripples on the water you might want to wait. Light air sailing can be fun and very challenging – but the boat will hardly be moving and it's hard to see the wind and feel how the boat and sails are reacting – not the perfect conditions for your first time. If the waves are big with *whitecaps* out on the open water – it is definitely too windy for your first solo sail. "Heavy air" sailing is super fun, especially in small boats – but small boats can *capsize* and to be able to handle that speed and extra force on the

sails and boat you will need some experience under your belt. For your first few solo trips – you don't want the wind speed to distract you from your focus of learning how to steer the boat and trim the sails.

In the following few pages you will be introduced to a sequence of steps that will help you learn to sail your boat. They are designed as practice drills to make things fun and easy on your first few sails. Each drill builds on the one before it. So, if the wind conditions are right – and there is some nice open water to practice in – let's go sailing!

Your first sail should be on a day when it is not too windy and not too light. Nice steady moderate winds are the most fun for now.

Start on a *beam reach* for getting the feel of sailing and beginning to practice trim and steering.

STARTING OUT: BEAM REACHING

Since you have been regularly noting the wind direction before casting off you should have a really good feel for it. The easiest point of sail to start with is a *beam reach* – sailing across the wind – in between the *no sail zone* and the *run*. Let's focus on mastering this point of sail first. The driver should be sitting on the "high" (*windward*) side of the boat. Both the *tiller* and the *mainsheet* should be in someone's hands (on a small boat one person can do both). If you are sailing on a *starboard tack beam reach* – with the wind blowing over the boat's right side – then the driver would be sitting on the right side of the boat. On every point of sail this driving position is important for visibility and to help you more easily control the boat's angle of *heel* (the amount the boat "leans over" in the wind.

Many boats have a *hiking stick* (*tiller* extension) that will allow the driver to sit outboard more – or even *hike out* (lean out over the side of the boat). When sitting to *windward*, if you are driving hold the *tiller* extension and steer with your *aft* (back) hand. So, if you are on a *starboard tack* you would hold the *hiking stick* with your left hand. That way your *forward* (right) hand is free to hold the *mainsheet*.

Once on a reaching course – pull the sail(s) in using the sheet(s) so they are not flapping (*luffing*) and get the feel of steering the boat with a *tiller* by using a distant reference point to gauge your heading. Once the boat gets moving it will be quite responsive to *tiller* movement, so keep a "soft" touch on the helm and keep the *tiller* close to the *centerline* to avoid any radical turns.

PRACTICE SAIL TRIM

As you sail comfortably on a *beam reach*
it is time to look up at the sails. You will
develop a habit of looking at the sails
regularly to see how they are trimmed. Your
attention should be constantly shifting
between the sails, the water *ahead* of the
boat, and the wind direction.

If you hold a steady course on a *beam reach*
the rudiments of sail trim will come easily. As
you adjust the sail trim – the sail's power and
the boat's *heel* will change and the *tiller* will
"pull" and the boat will want to turn, so keep
watching the horizon in front of the boat and
make small corrections with the *tiller* to keep
on a *beam reaching* course. For this sail trim
drill we will keep things simple and assume
the boat has only a *mainsail*. And although
some boats have a variety of "fine tuning" sail
trim controls (e.g. *cunningham*, *traveler*,
outhaul etc.) – the primary and most
important aspect of sail trim is controlled by
the *mainsheet*. The angle of the sail to the
wind direction is controlled by the *sheet* – the
fundamental sail trim control.

REMEMBER In this drill we focus on the
sheet's effect on sail trim. We assume that
the *luff* and *foot* of the *mainsail* is tensioned
(by the *halyard*, *cunningham* and *outhaul*)
just enough to remove any wrinkles. If your
boat has an adjustable *traveler* – secure it
on *centerline*. These are good "average"
settings for these fine tuning controls.

① **Flap the mainsail:** When the boat is
moving along at a good speed, release the
mainsheet completely; the sail will begin
flapping like a flag. Keep steering straight
and move your body slightly to *leeward* if
the boat *heels* to *windward* too much.
Without the driving force from the full sail,
the boat will begin to slow down and
eventually stop. It's quite valuable to be

WIND

FLAPPING SAIL – VERY SLOW

able to stop the boat in a controlled
manner – and as long as the boat is still on
a *beam reaching* course – then you are in
control and ready to easily get going again.

TIP *This is the* safety position – *with the sail
fully* luffing/*flapping the boat drifts along very
slowly on a beam or* close reach.

② **Half Trim:** Keep steering straight on a
beam reach! Pull in the *mainsheet* a few feet

HALF TRIM, SOME LUFFING – SLOW

PERFECT TRIM – FAST

until the sail begins to fill. Watch the sail carefully and notice how it stops flapping and fills at the back edge first. Stop trimming the *sheet* when the sail is "half full" with the back half of the sail catching wind, while the front edge (by the *mast*) is still "bubbling" (*luffing*). Notice as the sail fills that the *heel* of the boat will change and the boat will want to *head up* (turn toward the wind). With small *tiller* movements you can keep the boat straight on a *beam reach* and the crew can move their weight slightly to reduce

the *heel*. At "half trim", the boat will pick up some speed – but you can go faster.

③ **Full Trim:** Stay on a *beam reach*. Trim the *sheet* slowly until the "bubble" at the front edge **just** disappears and the sail looks smooth and "full". This is perfect sail trim for maximum power – set right on the "edge" of seeing that "bubble" – and the boat will accelerate to full speed. Practice easing the *sheet* out a few inches until you see a "bubble" and then re-trim until the *luffing* at the front edge of the sail just disappears.

STEERING

Keep watching the horizon or the land *ahead* of you to help you hold a steady *beam reaching* course. Notice how every time the boat goes over a wave or feels a change in wind speed, the *tiller* "pulls" slightly (one way or the other) and the boat wants to turn. It's like driving a bicycle or car on a bumpy road – you constantly have to make small steering corrections with the *tiller* to keep a straight course. You will also notice that moving the crew's body weight across the boat one way or the other will cause the boat to change its angle of *heel* and cause the boat to want to turn one way or another. For now – try to keep the boat level or flat – with no *heel* so you can focus on maintaining a straight course on a *beam reach*. If you have a crew on board – they should be sitting *forward* of the driver. They should adjust their position to keep the boat flat (not heeled) so the driver can stay comfortable sitting on the *windward* side and concentrating on driving.

....

TIP *Assuming you are on* port tack *and sitting to* windward *– push the* tiller *to the right to turn left and pull it to the left to turn right.*

....

PRACTICE TURNING

After you have straight line sailing under your belt it's time to get a feel for how much to move the *tiller* to get the boat to turn. Make some small "S" turns – only turn back and forth about 10 degrees. No big turns yet – avoid the *no sail zone* and the downwind point of sail. If you keep your turns small – the sail(s) will keep powering the boat without need of readjustment even though their trim is not "perfect". We just want to focus on steering first.

WIND

Get the feel of turning with the *tiller* by making some small turns centered around a *beam reaching* course.

Notice how the boat turns toward the wind (*heads up*) if you push the *tiller* away from you (toward the side of the boat the sails are on). Also note that if you let go of the *tiller* the boat will likely not go straight, it will usually *head up*. Like a car or bicycle that is out of balance and "wants" to turn one way – this *weather helm* is a characteristic of most sailboats.

SAIL TRIM ON OTHER POINTS OF SAIL

The basic rules of sail trim on a *beam reach* apply on all *points of sail* except the most downwind section of *broad reaching* and *running*. On those downwind angles, the sail is in drag mode – working less like a

wing – with air flow streaming across it – and more like a parachute blocking the wind. Here, the sail cannot *luff* so simply set your trim with the *mainsheet* so that the *boom* is perpendicular to the wind direction.

Congratulations! You have now learned the basics of sailing on a *reach*. Now all you have to do is refine these techniques of steering and sail trim. Once you have the *beam reach* under control try *heading up* to a *close reach* and then *heading down* to a *broad reach* and re-trimming the sails appropriately as shown below.

REMEMBER Pay attention to the wind direction. Any turn toward the wind is called *heading up* and any turn away from the wind is called *heading down* or *bearing away*/off.

WIND

SAIL TRIM ON A CLOSE REACH

WIND

SAIL TRIM ON A BROAD REACH

UNDER TRIMMED
– SLOW, LOW
SAIL POWER

WIND

OVER TRIMMED
– SLOW, EXCESS
HEEL

WIND

PROPER TRIM
– FAST, MAX SAIL
POWER

WIND

SAIL TRIM FOR SPEED

You now know how to look for the *luffing* at the front edge of a sail to trim for maximum power. The problem is that a sail can look full when it is trimmed in too tight. It is only by constantly testing the trim that you know if the sail is properly trimmed. Testing the trim can be done by either slightly easing the *mainsheet* while holding a steady course or by *heading up* until you see that small bubble or *luffing* in the front of the sail.

Even without looking for the *luffing* you can get the sail trimmed close to perfection by considering the wind direction and your point of sail. In general, trim the sail tight for *close-hauled* "upwind" sailing, ease it out about halfway (let out a few feet of *mainsheet*) when *beam reaching*, and let the *sheet* out a lot – so the sail or *boom* is perpendicular to the wind and *hull* when *broad reaching* or *running* downwind.

....

TIP *Overtrimming a sail is a common error. When in doubt – let it out!*

....

STEERING FOR FULL SPEED

The key of steering fast is to settle on a steady course with the sail well-trimmed for that point of sail. Remember you will constantly make small *tiller* "corrections" to keep going straight because many forces (wind, waves, *heel*) will push the *bow* and boat around. Watch the horizon *ahead* to help hold a steady course.

STEERING AND TRIMMING TO SLOW DOWN

The best way to slow down is to take the power out of the sail. To practice this, turn to a *close reach* or *beam reach* (you want to avoid getting stuck in the *no sail zone*) and then ease the *mainsheet* until the sail is half full. If you want to slow down more, release the *mainsheet* until the sail is fully flapping. Remember this is the *safety position* where you can drift along going slowly *forward* with little sail power and still have some steering control with the *rudder*. When you do trim the sail to get going again, the boat's balance will change. Pay close attention to your course and steer to avoid an unwanted turn toward the *no sail zone*!

It's impossible to slow down when sailing downwind because you cannot release the *mainsheet* enough for the sail to *luff* and lose power. To slow down from a *broad reach* or *run*, simply turn the boat to a *close* or *beam reach*, and then ease the sail out to reduce power as shown here.

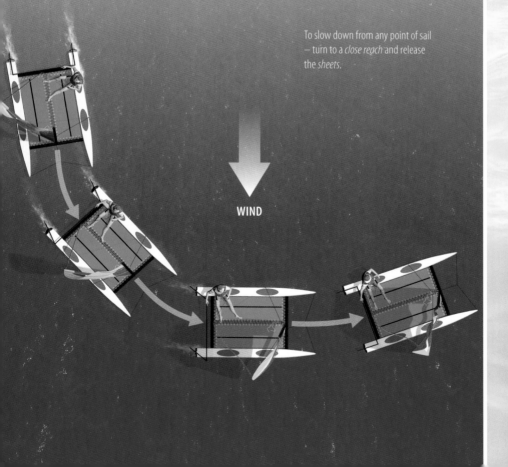

To slow down from any point of sail — turn to a *close reach* and release the *sheets*.

WIND

SAILING UPWIND – CLOSE-HAULED

Sailing upwind is a really fun point of sail, and it is fundamentally different from all the other reaching *points of sail* because the driver must do more than just hold a steady course.

CONCENTRATE ON STEERING

Sailing upwind, the sails get pulled in tight and it's up to the driver to concentrate and keep the boat moving *forward* – right on the edge of the *no sail zone*. Since the wind is never 100 percent steady – this requires continual small course changes to keep the boat sailing efficiently. On this point of sail, if there's good wind, the boat will want to *heel* so make sure everyone is sitting on the high (*windward*) side. The goal is to reduce *heel* and keep the boat flat, with the *mast* pointed straight up or just slightly away from the wind. *Close-hauled* sailing requires very smooth and accurate steering. Remember, just keep a nice, easy touch on the *tiller* and avoid oversteering.

On any *reaching* point of sail, you picked a heading and adjusted sail trim to that course. But sailing *close-hauled* you will trim the sails in tightly and then delicately alter your course to keep the sails just full. Once you find that magic "*groove*" where the tightly trimmed sails are just about to *luff*, you try to keep the boat steering very straight – only changing course when the wind shifts. *Telltales* on the *jib* really help.

The crew has trimmed and cleated the *jib* for good upwind trim. Now the driver watches the *telltales* and water *ahead* of the boat, feels the *heel* and pressure on the *tiller* and *mainsheet* and tries to sail in the "*groove*"

It's easy to drift off a *close-hauled* course and out of the "*groove*" if you are not careful. If you *bear away* unintentionally the sails will continue to appear full and the boat will move (albeit slightly more slowly) even if you turn down to a *beam reaching*

CLOSE-HAULED

WIND

IN THE "GROOVE" SAILING UPWIND

KEYS TO UPWIND SAILING

■ Pay attention to the wind direction – remember it is rarely constant.

■ Trim in the *mainsheet* tight – and keep it held steady – use the *cleat* if it's pulling too hard – but keep the *sheet* in your hand.

■ Don't over*heel*. Use crew weight to control the boat's *heel* angle.

■ Steer so the sail is just about to show a small *luff* in the front edge.

■ Look at the horizon *ahead* and pick a point to help steer straight. Feel the wind on your cheeks!

■ Check your upwind course frequently by turning toward the wind slowly until you see the bubble in the sail and then *bear away* just enough so the bubble disappears.

■ Keep your boat speed up – slowing down so close to the *no sail zone* risks getting stuck *in irons*. If you feel slow, *bear away* a few degrees to speed up.

course. The solution is to be aware of the wind direction and occasionally test that you are sailing as close to the wind as possible by *heading up* until you see the sails begin to *luff*.

It's even easier to get out of the groove with an unintentional turn toward the wind. But then the warning signs will be quite obvious. The sails will *luff* and the boat will quickly slow down. Before the boat comes to a stop (remember, without *forward* motion the boat cannot be turned), pull the *tiller* gently toward you (the *windward* side of the boat) to *bear away*. It shouldn't take much of a turn to get back on course, in the *groove* and up to speed.

Another common mistake when sailing *close-hauled* is easing the sails out. Since your sail trim constrains how close to the wind your boat can sail, the *sheet*(s) should be pulled tight. The exception is in windy conditions when you may have to ease – to *luff* the *mainsail* and avoid excessive *heel*.

TELLTALES

Short strands of dark yarn or ribbon (telltales) taped on either side of the lower front edge of any sail or on the *shrouds* a little above eye level can help you find and stay in that upwind *groove* (and they help with sail trim on *reaches* too). They work better on a *jib* than a *mainsail* because there is no *mast* disturbing the air flow. They are even more sensitive indicators of the wind flow over the sail than the "bubble" in the *luff*.

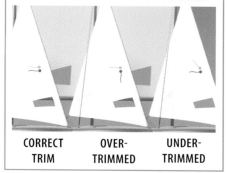

| CORRECT TRIM | OVER-TRIMMED | UNDER-TRIMMED |

CHANGING TACKS

Until now, you've been focusing on sailing on different *points of sail* on the same *tack*. At some point, you are going to want to go back in the other direction, and that requires changing course so much that the wind will blow on the other side of the boat.

COMING ABOUT/TACKING

To change tacks, you have two choices – turn upwind through the *no sail zone* (*tacking*) or bear way downwind past the *running* point of sail (*jibing*). Either way you do it, these maneuvers take practice and action on the boat. You will be turning the *tiller*, moving your body to the other side of the boat and trimming the sails on the new course.

Technically, a boat can *tack* from any point of sail to the other side of the *points of sail* circle. For example, we could *tack* from a *starboard tack broad reach* to a *port tack beam reach*. But that would be a really big turn! To make things easier, focus on *tacking* from *close-hauled* on one *tack* to *close-hauled* on the other *tack* – a turn of about 90 degrees. So, if we were on a

starboard tack broad reach – we would first *head up* to *starboard tack close-hauled*, get the sails trimmed so the boat is moving *forward* and then begin our *tack*.

By changing tacks, you can now sail to a destination that is directly upwind by criss-crossing. Christopher Columbus would have been envious because his ancient sailing ships could barely sail "higher" than a *beam reach* making an upwind destination nearly out of reach! *Tacking* is an easy maneuver. It requires a fairly big turn (about 90 degrees) to get from one *close-hauled* course to the other. When ready to commence the turn, push the *tiller* to *leeward* – away from you assuming that you are sitting on the *windward* side. The driver must also change sides of the boat during the "*tack*" to steer from the "new" *windward* side. In a boat with a *jib* the crew will work together with the driver by also changing sides of the boat while shifting the *jib* from one side to the other.

TIP *For the driver, learning to* tack *is sort of like learning a dance step because you must keep one hand on the* tiller/hiking stick *passing it behind your back, and one on the* mainsheet *as you change sides. Once on the new side you can switch hands so once again the* aft *hand is holding the* tiller/hicking stick *and the* forward *hand is holding the* mainsheet *(unless you have a crew handling the* mainsheet*).*

COMMON MISTAKES

Here are several common mistakes to avoid when *tacking*:

■ Not turning the boat fast or far enough and getting stuck *in irons* – with the boat pointing directly toward the wind.

■ Letting out the *mainsheet* substantially.

■ Turning the boat too much so it ends up on a *reach* instead of *close-hauled* on the new *tack*.

■ On a boat with a *jib* – forgetting to uncleat and retrim the *jib sheet* on the new side.

■ Not ducking your head as you cross to the other side and hitting it on the *boom*.

■ Not moving to the other side – or ending up in some contorted, ridiculous looking position.

STEPPING THROUGH A TACK

① Start out on a *close-hauled* heading with good speed. Speed is your friend in a *tack*! Look over your *windward* shoulder for a visual reference about 90 degrees from your course. This will help you know when/where to stop turning after tacking.

② Before turning, prepare the crew and announce your turn by saying something like "ready to *tack*". When everyone is ready you can start the process by saying something like "*tacking* now".

③ Push the *tiller* to *leeward* to start the turn. You want to commit to a fairly quick turn – so the boat doesn't get stopped while passing through the *no sail zone*. Keep the *mainsheet* in tight.

④ When the boat is pointed directly toward the wind and the sail is *luffing* – begin to move your body across the boat.

⑤ As the boat exits the no-sail zone slow down your turn and move to your new upwind sailing position.

⑥ Stop your turn when the sails fill. Get back into the *groove* on the new *tack*.

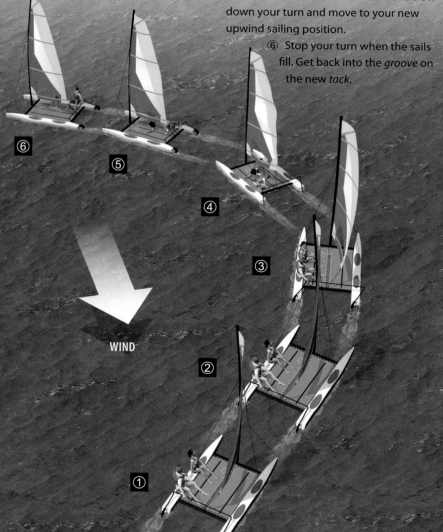

WIND

GETTING STUCK IN IRONS AND GETTING OUT

Although we sailors try to avoid the *no sail zone*, there are times, especially on a catamaran, when you will get "stuck" here. The sails will be flapping and cannot power the boat *forward*. The boat will slow down and stop – and eventually move backward. Getting stuck *in irons* can only happen when you stay too long in the *no sail zone*.

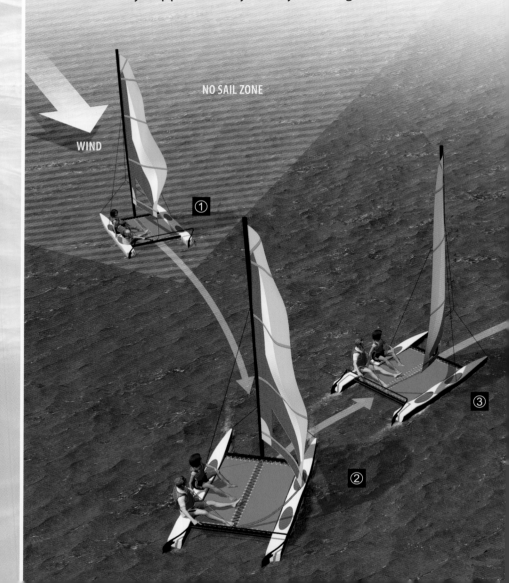

NO SAIL ZONE

WIND

①

②

③

HOW TO AVOID GETTING STUCK IN IRONS:

■ Keep your boat speed up with good sail trim and by steering outside the *no sail zone*.

■ When you do pass through the *no sail zone* (like when *tacking*), turn through quickly, keeping some speed for steering control.

....

TIP *If your boat has a* jib – *it can help you get out of irons. Once stuck, follow the steps above and simply trim the* jib *sheet tight on the opposite side of where your* tiller *is pointing – as the boat rotates the wind will push on the sail and help turn the boat out of the* no sail zone.

....

HOW TO GET OUT OF IRONS

Stuck *in irons*? You must "back" out of it – letting the wind push the boat backwards until the *rudder* starts working in "reverse".

① Push the *tiller* all the way in the direction you want the *bow* to go and hold it there. (If you want to sail off on *port tack*, push the *tiller* all the way to the right.)

Release the *mainsheet* fully and keep it really loose and uncleated so the boat can rotate out of the *no sail zone* without having the sail catch wind and fill. Keep the *mainsail* flapping.

② Keep the *tiller* pushed hard over – do not move it yet. Slowly the boat will begin rotating toward the left, pushed backwards by the wind.

③ Once the *bow* is pointed well out of the *no sail zone* (at least on a close reaching course) then slowly trim the sail until it fills halfway and then pull the *tiller* a bit past *centerline* to avoid *heading up*.

As the boat begins to move *forward* the wind will try to turn it back up to the *no sail zone*. Pay attention and use the *tiller* to stay on a close or *beam reach*. Boat speed is your friend.

④ Trim the sail more until it is full and perfectly trimmed. You are free!

This boat is *in irons* but, with the *tiller* held to one side, the boat will eventually blow backwards and turn out of the *no sail zone*.

SAILING DOWNWIND

Sailing downwind on a *broad reach* is a great point of sail – especially when it's windy. The boat really surfs along on the waves and, because the wind is from behind, you rarely get wet. Just keep in mind that what goes down must come up. If you sail downwind for a mile you will have to sail back upwind about a mile and a half (because you will have to *tack*). It can be difficult to distinguish between a *broad reach* and a *running* point of sail – but because of the dangers of an accidental *jibe* when sailing *by the lee* it's best to avoid sailing on a *run* – especially in shifty and stronger winds.

SAIL TRIM

Sail trim is pretty simple when sailing downwind. Just let the mainsail out all the way until it touches the *shroud* or when the *boom* is perpendicular to the wind, if the boat has no *shrouds*. A *jib* will not be very effective since the *mainsail blocks* the wind. For fun, you may want to try to *wing* the *jib* by holding it out on the opposite (*windward*) side from the main.

You will find that on a *broad reach* or *run* you can sit more inside the boat to keep it upright. And the *centerboard* – which you leave down all the way for the upwind and close reaching *points of sail* – can be raised a bit – say 1/3 of the way to improve performance. Another sail control that comes in handy on downwind *points of sail* is the *boom vang*. When sailing downwind in medium or strong breeze the *vang* should be tensioned to keep the *boom* from soaring way up in the air. By keeping the *boom* down, the back edge (*leech*) of the *mainsail* can stay straight – presenting more area to the wind and making the sail shape more like a wing.

Sailing downwind with moderate *boom vang* tension and a "winged" *jib*.

WIND

Sailing downwind in good form, *mainsail* eased, *boom vang* taught, *daggerboard* slightly raised.

ACCIDENTAL JIBE

When sailing on a *reach* you have more margin for straying off course compared with the accuracy needed to steer the boat in the "*groove*" when sailing *close-hauled*. But as you *bear away* onto a *broad reach* or *run* – your attention to the wind direction and your boat's heading should become focused again. This is because of the danger of the accidental *jibe* which occurs when the wind catches the *mainsail* on its back side and flings the *boom* and sail across rapidly. An accidental *jibe* can be startling at best and downright dangerous at worst. Any body part above the plane of the *boom* zinging across is at risk. Some sailors wear a helmet for protection. Sailing *by the lee* causes this dangerous situation. It can be brought on by careless steering or just an unexpected wave or wind shift that brings the wind direction to the wrong side of the boat. The best way to prevent an accidental *jibe* is to avoid sailing directly downwind on a *run* and limit your downwind point of sail to a deep *broad reach*. This is a wise rule – especially in stronger wind. Keeping track of the wind direction will help you avoid sailing *by the lee*.

(BEFORE) BY THE LEE

WIND

(AFTER) An accidental jibe is embarassing at best and can be dangerous.

JIBING

A jibe is another way to change tacks – but it's done by turning the boat away from the wind. During a jibe the *boom/mainsail* swings across rapidly from one side to the other – so keep your head low. In strong winds – the forces during a jibe can be so violent that it is better to *tack* instead (informally called a "chicken jibe").

TO TACK OR JIBE?

Your choice of whether to change tacks by *coming about* or jibing will be dictated by your current point of sail, the conditions and your destination. If there is a nice gentle breeze and you are sailing on a *broad reach* and have a destination that is farther downwind – then a jibe may be in order since it will require a lot less turning than *heading up* and *tacking*.

STEPPING THROUGH A JIBE

For ease of control and to minimize your turn – start out on a *broad reaching* course – neither a *beam reach* nor a *run*. Pick a spot on the horizon that will be your *broad reaching* course on the "new" *tack* (about a 30-degree turn). Announce something like "stand by to jibe" to prepare the crew then, when ready, announce "jibing".

COMMON MISTAKES

Common mistakes to avoid when jibing:
- ■ Not preparing the crew so that they are ready and in a safe position when the *mainsail* and *boom* come flying across.
- ■ Not changing sides as the *boom* comes across so that the boat becomes unstable.
- ■ Not ducking low enough and not being aware of the path of the *mainsheet* and *boom vang* as the sail jibes. If you stay in your normal sailing position — your head would get hit every jibe.
- ■ Not pulling in the *mainsail* as you start the turn — causing the *boom* to jibe across later and with more force. This is a recipe for a *capsize*.

WIND

①

① Start your turn (*bearing away*) by pulling the *tiller* toward you. Don't turn as far or fast as in a *tack*.

② Begin to pull in the *mainsheet* fairly quickly and keep your head low. Begin to move your body to the new side. As the boat turns past "dead downwind' the *mainsail* feels wind on the "new" side and flies across with a bang. You should time your move across the boat so that you are getting to the new *windward* side just as the *mainsail* fills.

③ Straighten out your course on the new *broad reach* and ease the *mainsheet* back out for proper sail trim.

REMEMBER In stronger winds the jibe is a tricky maneuver. What was, in light air, an easy matter of throwing the *boom/mainsail* across can become a real challenge in strong winds. The possibility of capsizing, although always present in a *centerboard* boat, is at its highest during a jibe in strong winds. So, there is no one who will fault you if you decide to *tack* in lieu of jibing. Remember, you never have to jibe. As you gain more experience and confidence you will be able to jibe in stronger and stronger winds. But a jibe in windy conditions will always be one of the most exciting moments of small boat sailing.

③

②

REVIEW QUESTIONS (see page 96 for answers)

CHOOSE FROM THE ANSWERS PROVIDED

1 What does NOT need to be done before sailing? (Choose all correct answers)

a Make sure you have your life jacket and other sailing gear

b Keep your eye out for power wires when rigging and moving your boat

c Inspect the fittings holding the mast and shrouds in place

d Make sure sails are completely dry

e Make sure hull and buoyancy tanks are drained and plugged tightly

2 Why do you want to tie up the boat at a dock so that it points directly toward the wind? (Choose all correct answers)

a So that no one can hit your boat

b To make it easy to hoist your sails

c So that the boat does not hit the dock while you are rigging the sails

d To practice your knots

e It is easiest to start sailing on a run

3 Answer the following statements "True" or "False".

a Jib and main halyards should never be pulled tight

b Main sheets and jib sheets should never be cleated when the boat is sitting at the dock

c Winds over 15 knots are recommended for your first sail

d The "no sail zone" where one gets stuck in irons and the angle one sails "by the lee" are the same direction

e If a sail is not luffing, then it is properly trimmed

f Once you set the sail trim you never change it

4 The difference in sail trim between close-hauled sailing and other points of sail is: (choose the best answer).

a When sailing close-hauled you keep the sails trimmed tightly (except in strong breezes) and steer carefully to keep them from luffing b Telltales only work for points of sail other than close-hauled

c The sail generates more power when sailing close-hauled

d You do not have to look up at the luff of the sail when sailing close-hauled

e It is easier to do

5 When sailing on a broad reach – the best way to slow down and take a rest is to: (choose the best answer)

a Overtrim the sails

b Drag your arms in the water

c Head the boat up to a beam reach and trim in the sails

d Head the boat up to a beam reach and ease the sails

e Jibe the boat to a broad reach on the other tack

6 To get better sail trim while on a beam reach you should look up at the front of the sail and ... (choose all correct answers)

a If the sail looks like a flag – completely flapping – trim in the sail by pulling in on its sheet until the sail looks completely full

b If the sail looks completely full you have perfect trim already

c If the sail looks completely full you should slowly ease the sheet until you just see a small bubble and then retrim the sheet until the bubble just disappears

d If the sail has a small bubble in the leading edge slowly trim in the sail until the bubble disappears

7 You are sailing on a broad reach on port tack and want to change tacks and sail on a broad reach on starboard tack. Should you tack or jibe? (Choose all the best answers)

a You should do whatever you want to – it's a free world

b If the wind and/or wave conditions make jibing dangerous because of the risk of capsize then you should tack

c If the wind is light to moderate and the seas are flat – easy conditions for risk-free jibing, you should jibe because it's easier and a smaller turn

d Any time you think jibing would risk a capsize, then you should tack

e You should just keep going straight on port tack and avoid any turns

CHAPTER 3
Safe sailing

CAPSIZING

Capsizing is a part of sailing small boats. It can be a nuisance, but it should never be feared. Given proper preparation and practice it can be handled easily. Although a *capsize* can be frustrating, it can also be fun. If the water is warm you may appreciate the opportunity to cool off.

PRACTICE THE "FLIP"

Sooner or later you are going to "flip", so why not now? Just like every sailor should wear a *life jacket* – every sailor learning to sail small boats should practice capsizing the boat. Practice on a nice day in light winds near a shore or a dock with a rescue boat standing by.

With the boat flipped upside down, all of the loose gear in the boat might float away, so plan ahead and make sure everything is well secured or tied into the boat. When it comes to capsizing, there are two types of boats – those that can be righted and sailed dry (self-righting/self-bailing) and those that "swamp", fill with water and require outside assistance to recover. The difference is in the boat's design and whether it has sealed flotation tanks. You should avoid sailing a "*swamper*" if there is no rescue boat. Catamarans and many modern dinghies are always self-bailing.

Capsizing is part of small boat sailing – and it can be fun!

ANATOMY OF A CAPSIZE

Capsizes usually occur in strong winds – although if you are careless – you could *capsize* a dinghy in no wind at all. There are two ways a boat can *capsize* while sailing: by tipping over to *leeward* (*mast* rotates downwind – away from the boat) or to *windward* (*mast* rotates over the boat). A *leeward capsize* is common in strong or puffy winds when the boat simply "blows over" because the crew did not sit out on the side (*hike*) and/or ease the *mainsheet* enough. A catamaran almost always *capsizes* to *leeward* – either in the aforementioned manner – or by "*pitchpoling*" when going fast and the *bow* digs too deep into the waves. Moving the crew weight farther back in the boat can prevent *pitchpoling*.

WIND

LEEWARD CAPSIZE

HOW TO AVOID A CAPSIZE

■ Don't sail on windy days until you are ready to handle a *capsize* and have enough experience.
■ Avoid *jibing* in strong winds – *tack* instead.
■ Never *cleat* the *mainsheet*. Quickly releasing the *mainsheet* as the boat starts to *heel* too much will take the power out of the sails.
■ Don't sit on the boat's *leeward* side. If on *starboard tack*, sit on the right (*windward*) side of the boat.

■ When sailing on a *close reach* or *close-hauled* point of sail – if you feel the boat starting to go – release the *mainsheet* and turn upwind toward the *no sail zone* to reduce power.
■ When *broad reaching* or running in a dinghy, if you feel the boat rocking and starting to death roll – trim in the *mainsheet* a few feet and turn upwind about 20 degrees to gain control.

IF YOU CAPSIZE

- Don't panic – it's just water
- Make sure everyone is safe
- Do all you can to keep the *mast* horizontal to the water – not pointed straight down

WIND

WINDWARD CAPSIZE

WINDWARD CAPSIZE

The other common *capsize* scenario on a dinghy is turning over to *windward*. This will occur in strong winds when sailing downwind, especially during a *jibe*, or on any point of sail when the body weight is too far to *windward* in relation to the amount of wind. The boat just starts rolling back and forth and finally ... the "death roll". A death roll is less common than a leeward *capsize* because it can be avoided by *heading up* to a *reach* and trimming the *mainsheet*. And if you do need to go the other way – simply *tack* instead of *jibe*.

When the boat flips to leeward, the crew's first reaction is to stay dry and climb over the high side and onto the *centerboard* (or lower *hull* of a catamaran). This "walkover method" or "dry *capsize*" is the

proper reaction but it must be done quickly. Most boats do not like to float on their sides; they prefer to roll belly up with the *mast* pointing straight down. This ignoble position is known as the "turtle". Because of the difficulty of righting a fully inverted catamaran, most cats have a large float on the top of the *mast* that prevents a turtle. To prevent a turtle on a dinghy get on to the *centerboard* quickly when the boat is still on its side. But if you spend too much time climbing over the side you will accelerate the turtleing process. The other choice, and sometimes it's the only choice, is to jump into the water and swim around to the exposed *centerboard* (or *hull* of a catamaran). This is when you will be happy that you are wearing a *life jacket* because it is difficult to swim with your clothes on.

RIGHTING THE CAPSIZED BOAT

If the boat has turtled – with the *mast* fully under the water and pointed straight down, this process will be done in three steps.
① The first is to use your body weight and leverage by standing or holding onto the *centerboard* to rotate the boat so the *mast* and sail are lying parallel and on top of the water. This process can take time as the sails come up through the water so be patient and keep pulling as long as the boat is showing signs of rolling up.

REMEMBER If you can prevent the boat from turtleing – righting the boat will be much easier and faster.

Once the boat is resting on its side – make

CAPSIZE RULE # 1

Always stay with the boat. If you *capsize* and cannot right it, don't try to swim to shore. By staying with the boat, you can be seen better, float longer and be rescued sooner.

① ② ③

WIND

RIGHTING A DINGHY

certain that the *sheets* are uncleated and free to run and your crew is safe and happy.

② On a dinghy simply pull (or stand) on the *centerboard* of a mono*hull* and use your body weight to bring the boat upright. On a catamaran use a *"righting line"* rigged under the *trampoline* (or rig a *sheet* or other *line* from the "top" *hull* to give you something to pull on) to lean out to lever the boat upright. A crew can help out the righting process by providing extra leverage on the *righting line* or *centerboard*.

③ As long as the *mainsheet* and *jib sheets* are uncleated, and the *bow* is pointed in or near the *no sail zone*, the boat will hopefully remain upright while you pull yourself in.

WIND

RIGHTING A CATAMARAN

WIND

① ②

THE SCOOP METHOD

If there are two or more sailors – this method makes it easy for one of them to get pulled into the dinghy as it comes upright.

① One crew prevents the boat from turtleing by keeping pressure on the *centerboard* while the other swims to the opposite side and ensures the *sheets* are uncleated and free to run. Then they grab the hiking strap at the helm position and yell to the other crew to right the boat.

② The swimming crew gets scooped into the boat as it's righted making it easier to keep the boat under control while the rest of the crew member(s) climb in.

AVOIDING A "REFLIP"

When the boat is on its side – its orientation to the wind and waves is important. It is a lot easier to right the boat and keep it upright while you climb in if the *bow* is pointed between head to wind and a *close reach*. If the *mast* is to *windward* of the *hull* (often the case after a *death roll*) getting the boat to stay upright will be more challenging. This is because as you lever the boat upright – the wind will lift the sail and push to flip the boat over again on top of you!

To avoid this – if the *mast* is to *windward* of the *hull* – the crew can swim to the *bow* and hold on to it. The boat will then drift slowly until the *bow* is pointed upwind – making righting easier.

THE QUICK TOW METHOD

A *"quick tow"* requires the assistance of a motorboat with a capable driver and provides an effective method of bailing out about half of the water in a swamped sailboat so that the sailor can safely climb aboard and easily bail out the remaining water.

① Right the swamped boat and ensure the sails are lowered. Some boats will be unstable when full of water so you may not be able to climb aboard. If so, uncleat the *halyard* and lower the sail(s) before righting the boat.

② Securely attach a strong tow rope around the *mast* at deck level. The crew should hold on to the *transom* to help hold the boat upright with the *bow* higher than the *transom*. When ready give the okay to the motorboat to begin slowly moving *forward*. The water in the boat will start flowing out over the *transom*.

③ Soon the water level will be down enough so you can stop the tow and safely climb in the boat. Once aboard – start bailing with a bucket!

RESCUING THE "SWAMPER"

Dinghies without built-in flotation take more time to get sailing again. First you must lower the sails and bring the boat upright by pulling on the *centerboard* and *hull*. It will be lying very low in the water – with the *cockpit* completely full. Now you are faced with a big job of bailing. On a *"swamper"* it's wise to carry a big bucket or *bailer*.

Climb into the boat over the *transom* so it doesn't flip again and start bailing like crazy. If you are fast and keep the boat upright, you can slowly gain on the flood waters and get it dry. But, a boat half filled with water is very unstable and can easily flip again.

DON'T GO IT ALONE!

Never go out alone on a boat that is not self-rescuing. Always make sure there are other boats around and that you have a good bucket or *bailer* on board.

SAILING IN STRONGER WINDS

Sailing in strong breezes (15+ knots) can be an exhilarating experience in a small boat. There is nothing quite like flying along, inches above the water, with spray blasting all around the *hull*. Heavy air sailing requires practice. As a beginner you should avoid these stronger breezes until you have gained some experience in light and moderate winds. It won't take long to feel confident in stronger breezes. Then you will relish windy days rather than feel uncomfortable whenever *whitecaps* froth. Never sail a boat in heavy air unless you are able to right it from a *capsize*.

UPWIND AND REACHING – CONTROLLING HEEL

It can be a real challenge to try to minimize the *heeling* forces of the wind. Most dinghies and cats sail best with no more than 10 degrees of leeward *heel*. For a catamaran, sailing on a *reach* or upwind in moderate and strong winds, the *windward hull* can be lifted out of the water – but not excessively.

BODY POSITION

Leaning out with your butt hanging over the *windward* side of the boat (*hiking*) is a very effective way to reduce *heel*. The *hiking stick* and *mainsheet* will help provide support. Some boats have hiking straps which you can hook your toes under to help you lean farther out. Many catamarans and some high-performance dinghies have a *trapeze* system where the crew members can "stand" fully out from the *windward* side hanging in a harness from a wire on the *mast*. Trapezing gets the crew

weight even farther out than *hiking*. However, no matter what kind of boat you are on, you (and your crew) must at least sit on the *windward* side.

STEERING

Another anti-*heel* technique is steering. By *heading up* a few degrees closer to

WIND

25°

TOO MUCH HEEL, EASE THE MAINSHEET A FEW INCHES

the wind you can reduce the pressure on the sails, thereby reducing *heel*. This is sometimes called "*pinching*" or "*feathering*". You will find that through very small course adjustments you will be able to accurately control *heel*. When using this technique, the sails may begin to lightly *luff* along their leading edges but the back half of the sails should remain full. Avoid *heading up* so much that the sails are fully *luffing* – you don't want to get stuck *in irons* in strong winds!

In strong winds, the *sheets* should be in your hand, ready to ease in a puff. This crew is using a trapeze to reduce *heel*.

SAIL TRIM

Maybe the most effective way to reduce *heel* on these tighter *points of sail* is to simply ease the *mainsheet*. This must be done controllably so the *heel* is reduced but the boat still maintains speed. The beauty of this technique is that it is very fast and easy. If your boat has a *jib*, it can be left fully trimmed while the constantly adjusted *mainsail* balances the boat. In these conditions, it is best to keep the *mainsheet* in your hand for fast reaction.

By using a combination of these techniques, you will be able to sail *close-hauled* and tight *reaching* very efficiently even in strong winds. The goal is to settle on an acceptable amount of *heel* (around 10 degrees) and then keep the boat sailing along with good speed at that angle. Your own internal sense of balance can easily sense small changes in the boat's *heel* angle, which you can then control.

....

TIP *Although it may be fun in strong winds to let the catamaran* heel *excessively – so that the windward hull* is flying high over the water *– it will sail faster and in more control if the* heel *is limited so the* hull *is just a few inches above the water. This is called "flying a* hull".
....

SAILING DOWNWIND IN STRONG WINDS

This is when sailing in strong breezes can be a real joy. *Broad reaching* is fast and exhilarating – and usually drier than the "tighter" reaches. Remember, when it's breezy, avoid sailing on a *run* since the boat will be prone to an accidental *jibe* or "death roll" *capsize*. As with the "tighter" *points of sail*, you will be sitting out on the *windward* side and controlling *heel* with body weight, *mainsheet* and steering. The *heeling* forces won't be as powerful and in the waves – you may find the boat rocking excessively – drastically heeling over to *windward* and then coming flat. If so – get the boat stable by *heading up* a few degrees and trimming in the *mainsheet*.

....

TIP *When sailing downwind in strong winds make sure the* boom vang *is snug so the* mainsail *has a good wing shape making it easier to control* heel.
....

CREW OVERBOARD

It does happen. For one reason or a combination of reasons, someone goes "swimming". Getting quickly and safely back to the swimmer and getting them back on board is your goal. It's wise to practice crew overboard recovery techniques by using a cushion or floating object. Remember, with one less crew on board – it may be more difficult to sail the boat. But this is just when you need the best and most accurate control. Stay calm and act carefully.

WHAT TO DO

Here are the steps you should follow if a crew goes overboard:

■ Spread the word (if you have other crew still on board) by shouting something like "crew overboard".

■ Throw flotation to the swimmer – hopefully they are also wearing their *life jacket.*

■ Keep an eye on the swimmer.

■ Plan the best way to return quickly and safely considering the boat and conditions.

■ Approach the swimmer slowly and under control – on a *close reach* you can control speed without losing steerage.

■ Get the swimmer back on board.

There are several courses you can choose to turn the boat and get back to the swimmer. The method you choose should be the one that suits you and your situation best. For example, if you are on a catamaran in light winds and every time you *tack* – you get stuck *in irons* – then you should *jibe* to get back to the swimmer quickly. Ultimately – all the methods have similar features and requirements– you must get prepared – change *tacks* by *tacking* or *jibing* and then get to a position so you can be sailing on a *close reaching* course, easily controlling your speed with sail trim as you approach the swimmer.

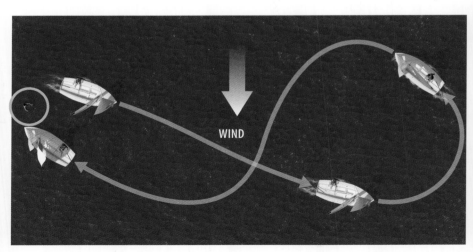

WIND

In the figure 8 method, you *tack* and then bear away so you can approach the swimmer slowly, with *luffing* sails on a *close reach.*

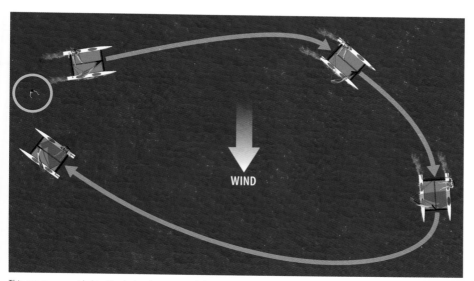

This catamaran avoided *tacking* by *bearing away* and *jibing* to approach the swimmer under control on a *close reach*.

SMART SAILOR'S RULES

■ Always wear a *lifejacket* (personal flotation device, or *PFD*). Find one that fits and is comfortable. In the US, the US Coast Guard (USCG) sets standards for *life jackets*. Make sure your *life jacket* is USCG-approved for your weight.

■ If your boat is 16' or longer – you must also bring a USCG-approved throwable device.

■ Always consider the weather forecast before sailing.

■ Set an upper limit for wind velocity. You have plenty of time to raise that limit as you gain experience.

■ Dress appropriately. Remember that it can be a lot colder on the water no matter how warm it is on shore.

■ Be sure of your ability to right the boat in case of a *capsize*. Make sure your buckets or *bailers* are tied into the boat so they will not float away.

■ Make sure your *rudder* will not fall out if the boat turns upside down.

■ Check and drain the tanks or *hulls* before sailing. Ensure they are sealed before launching.

■ The US Navy recommends whenever the sum of air and water temperature is less than 120 degrees, a wetsuit or similar protection should be worn.

■ Never stand between a floating boat and the shore if there are any waves.

■ Always keep a good lookout when sailing, especially in the "blind" spot to leeward underneath the *boom*.

■ Never go sailing when there are no other boats out.

■ Don't forget to duck when you *jibe*!

■ Make sure you have some way to get the boat ashore if the wind dies. Paddles work well on larger boats. You may be able to paddle with your hands on a smaller boat. A good trick is to aggressively rock the boat back and forth with the sails trimmed in tightly, "creating" your own wind.

■ Keep your hands and fingers in the boat when coming alongside a dock or another boat.

■ Head to shore immediately if there's thunder or lightning.

■ If you *capsize* and cannot right the boat, stay with the boat. Try to get out of the water by sitting on the overturned *hull* and wait for help.

■ Know the internationally recognized distress signal – repeatedly raise and lower your outstretched arms.

■ Consider bringing a knife – which can cut tangled ropes in an emergency.

WHAT TO WEAR

Remember, your lifejacket (*PFD*) should always be worn. Small boat sailing can be really wet. As a sailor, you should be even more focused on the water temperature and the "wind chill" factor than just the air temperature. On a summer day, shorts and a T-shirt may be the most comfortable shore-side attire. But out on the water the chilling effect of the wind and cold water on your body can cool you in a hurry. Fortunately, there is a lot of clothing designed specifically for the sailor and outdoor enthusiast to keep you comfortable in just about any condition.

DRESS FOR THE CONDITIONS

Let's start with your feet. Even on the warmest of days it is best to wear a pair of shoes to facilitate movement in the boat and protect yourself against injury from objects aboard the boat and in the water. There are a zillion "boat shoes" that dry quickly with non-skid rubber soles on the market but any pair of athletic shoes will work just as well. If it is cold, lightweight, low-profile neoprene boots designed for small boat sailing are a great option.

On a summer day – when the water is warm you can wear the same clothes you would on shore. However, it's a good idea to bring along a windbreaker or light shell jacket just in case things get a bit cool – and the long sleeves will help with sun protection. If the conditions (and especially the water temperature) are going to be a bit more frigid, you will need more gear. If you are going to get really wet (stronger winds) you might want some *foul weather gear* as your outside layer. Check out your

When the air and water are warm, a shirt, shorts, shoes and *life jacket* are a great sailing outfit.

When it's cold, wear layers and outer protection to stay dry.

local marine store – *foul weather gear* comes in all shapes and weights. For a small boat, you will be very active so make sure the gear is not too heavy and allows for a full range of movement. Add a layer or two of fuzzy clothing underneath for extra warmth – avoid cotton if you are going to get wet – wool or synthetics retain warmth better when damp. For boardsailing and real wet weather sailing a *wetsuit* or *drysuit* may be more appropriate. Ask local sailors and your instructor for advice on these specialty items. Many sailors like wearing sailing gloves or flexible gardening gloves to protect their hands when it's windy.

HYPOTHERMIA

Hypothermia is when your internal body temperature drops below 95 degrees F. Symptoms of mild hypothermia include feeling cold, violent shivering and slurred speech. Treatment includes wrapping the person in warm blankets and giving him/her warm fluids (no alcohol). Symptoms of moderate hypothermia include pale appearance, blue lips, headache, loss of muscular control, drowsiness, and incoherence. This is very serious. A person with moderate hypothermia needs to be immediately taken out of the cold and reheated. The best thing you can do to prevent hypothermia is to dress warmly. It may be warm on the dock or beach, but it's another situation out on the water in the spray and wind. Be prepared.

COPING WITH THE SUN

Most sailing is done in the warmer conditions where you can leave your *foul weather gear* ashore or rolled up in a plastic bag to stay dry on board. However, the harmful effects of the sun's ultraviolet rays are increased by the reflection off the sails and the water. A sunburn can ruin a nice day of sailing, sunscreen is essential. Most sailors wear hats and sunglasses with lenses that provide ultraviolet protection with polarization too. Heat exhaustion occurs when your body can't control its own temperature. Bring and drink fluids underway. If you feel sick, dizzy, tired or develop a headache, find help and a place to cool off.

Sunglasses and a hat help protect you from the sun.

REVIEW QUESTIONS (see page 96 for answers)

1 Answer the following statements "True" or "False".

a You should never practice capsizing in your boat because you know how to avoid capsizing

b Never sail a "swamper" without rescue boats around

c Always cleat the mainsheet before righting your boat

d You should cleat the mainsheet when sailing in heavy air because that's when it pulls the hardest

e It is good to sail with a lot of heel in strong winds

f Lifejackets should be taken off once away from land

g In strong winds it's ok to wait a few minutes to pick up an overboard crew

2 Which of the following are effective methods of reducing heel when sailing close-hauled in strong wind? (Choose all correct answers).

a Using a steering technique known as "pinching"

b Hiking out over the rail

c Sailing only on the tack that takes you toward land

d Moving from the windward side to the leeward side

e Easing the mainsheet and keeping the jib in tight

3 The best point of sail to approach and pick up a crew overboard is: (pick the best answer)

a In irons

b Close-hauled

c Close reach

d Beam reach

e Broad reach

4 The following techniques should be employed when sailing downwind in strong winds "True" or "False".

a Ease the boom vang to twist the mainsail

b Bear away in the puffs until you are sailing by the lee

c Move your crew weight forward in the boat to keep the bow in the water

d If the boat starts rolling head up to a broad reach to stabilize the angle of heel

5 Most small catamarans have a large float attached to the top of the mast because: (choose the best answer)

a It reduces windage and helps the boat tack

b It is extra storage for your personal gear

c It is a design feature that looks good

d To prevent a capsized cat from turning turtle because once inverted, a cat is very hard to self-right

6 The most important personal equipment to bring on a small boat is:

a Your foul weather gear

b A comfortable life jacket

c Sailing shoes

d Sun screen

e Extra rope and a knife

7 Answer the following statements "True" or "False".

a If it is very hot, you should remove your lifejacket to prevent heat exhaustion

b If you are wearing a wetsuit – you do not have to wear a life jacket

c You can't get sunburned on a cloudy day

d Sailing gloves help protect your hands when handling the sheets

e The best way to prevent hypothermia is to dress warmly and wear a waterproof outer layer

4

CHAPTER 4
Skills and concepts for every sailor

CREWING

Many small boats are designed to handle the extra weight and help of additional crew. Even a boat designed to be sailed by one person can be fun for two people. Just be careful not to excessively overload any boat. Crewing on 2-person and 3-person boats requires active participation in handling the boat.

ROLE OF THE CREW

The crew will be responsible for watching out for other boats and handling the *jib* if there is one. Other duties include: *hiking out*, moving their bodies to help balance the boat in a maneuver, adjusting the *centerboard* and control *lines* like the vang, looking for wind changes, helping to launch and dock the boat – and having fun!

Once sailing, it is especially important to be conscious of your position in the boat. Crew should be seated in front of the driver, moving from side to side to balance the boat. We have already pointed out the importance of sitting out on the *windward* side when it's windy – to counteract the heeling force of the wind. Because the crew does not have to steer, they are better able to move their weight to keep the boat in balance. In light winds this may mean sitting on the leeward side to counter the driver's weight so the boat is flat. REMEMBER Most dinghies sail best somewhere between flat (*mast* straight up, no *heel*) and 10 degrees of leeward *heel*. A catamaran is the same – you don't want the *hull* to fly too high out of the water.

Fore and *aft* weight placement is important too. In general, the driver and crew's combined weight should be centered around the *centerboard* in a dinghy or the middle of the *trampoline* on a cat. In light winds, slightly farther forward weight placement helps performance and when it's windy – shift the weight a foot or two, especially on a *reach* or a *run*.

This catamaran team is keeping their weight low and *forward* for best performance in light winds.

JIB TRIM

Jib trim is easy if you follow the sail trim rules introduced earlier. Simply stated, the sail must be trimmed (by the *jib sheet*) so that it looks full but is really on the verge of *luffing*. Since an over trimmed sail looks just as full as a perfectly trimmed one – the best way to check this is by slowly easing the *jib sheet* until the sail begins to show a very small amount of *luffing* and then retrim the *sheet* until the *luffing* just stops. However, when sailing *close-hauled*, the driver will

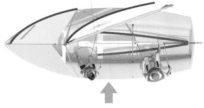 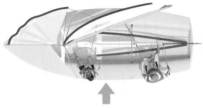

PERFECT TRIM

Both telltales streaming

UNDER TRIMMED

Windward telltale is dancing

perform this same "test" of trim by *heading up* slightly. When sailing *close-hauled*, simply trim the *jib sheet* tight and *cleat* it if possible – so the driver can better stay in that upwind *groove*. Here are four examples of *jib* trim on a *close reach*.

TIP Telltales *placed near the luff of the* jib *can really help the driver stay in the* groove *sailing upwind and can help the crew assess* jib *trim on any point of sail. Watch your sails closely for clues on how they should be trimmed.*

OVER TRIMMED

JIB ON WRONG SIDE

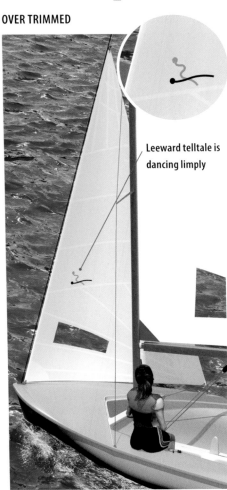

Leeward telltale is dancing limply

Telltales hanging down

CREWING DURING MANEUVERS

Changing *tacks* is an especially active time for the crew. Not only do they have to move to the opposite side of the boat in concert with the driver to keep the boat at the proper angle of *heel* – but they also must shift the tension from one *jib sheet* to the other. A common mistake is forgetting to change the *jib sheets* in a *tack* and ending up with the *jib* trimmed with the "wrong" (*windward*) *jib sheet*. If you get confused with *windward* and leeward just remember that the *jib* should always be trimmed with the leeward side *jib sheet* (except when *winging the jib* out when sailing downwind.) The easiest way to find the correct *jib sheet* is to fully release both *sheets* – the sail will flap like a flag with its back edge on one side of the *mast*. Pull in the *jib sheet* on that side. You can also look up at the *mainsail* and trim the *jib* to the same side.

On a catamaran with a *jib* the crew has plenty to do during a *tack*. Along with changing sides during the turn, they must also un*cleat* the "old" *jib sheet* and pull in the new one. Timing is key and practice makes perfect.

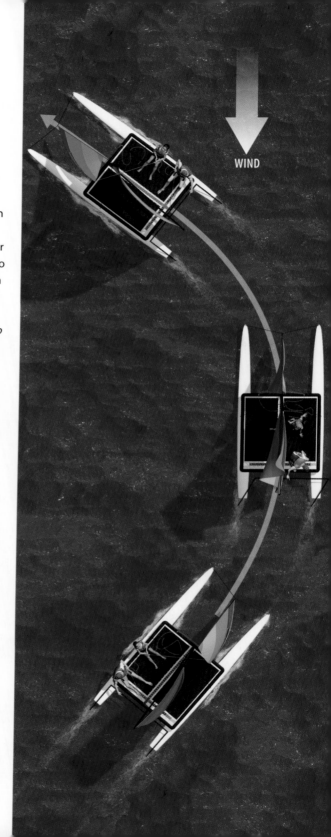

WIND

CENTERBOARD POSITION

When sailing *close-hauled*, the *centerboard* should be all the way down. The *centerboard* counteracts the sideways force created by the sails and allows the boat to move nearly straight *forward* instead of sliding sideways. When sailing downwind on a *broad reach*, the board can be raised a bit – about one-third to one-half at the most – which reduces drag but also makes the boat "tippier" – more unstable. As you head up, don't forget to put it back down again. Upwind performance will greatly decrease if the

Close-hauled: *Centerboard* should be fully down.

Broad reaching and *running*: *Centerboard* can be raised a bit to reduce drag.

centerboard is raised because the boat will slip sideways. When just learning to sail on a tippy monohull, even on a *run* – keep your *centerboard* all the way down for extra stability.

....

TIP Centerboard *position is not critical to downwind performance – when in doubt leave it down – that will provide a bit of extra stability and ensure you don't forget it when turning back upwind. Some catamarans are designed to sail well without any* centerboard. *Their long slender hulls resist side-slip when sailing upwind.*
....

PLANNING YOUR NEXT SAIL

Once you have learned enough to sail solo, you will be faced with the decision of where to go. There are several factors that you may want to consider when planning your sail. Although some of the best days are when you just "sail around" with no set plan, you still want to keep the following points in the back of your mind.

WIND AND WEATHER

You should always check the weather before sailing so that you are not caught out in a sudden squall or winds above your skill level. As a sailor, your interest in weather and the "marine weather forecast" greatly increases. Along with the big picture forecast – look for sailing-specific information (wind, waves and storms). There are several apps and websites that provide wind forecasts and information for popular sailing spots. In the US, NOAA provides marine forecasts for boaters available both on VHF radio and the internet. Getting a good forecast should be the foundation of your weather preparation.

Plan your day to maximize your chances of a nice sailing breeze and to avoid sailing in stronger winds than you are capable of handling. On warm summer days, many places where you sail experience a *sea breeze*. This "onshore" breeze blows from the water toward the shore and picks up throughout the daylight hours. You may want to plan your sail for the best breeze of the day – or in windy areas – you might opt to go sailing before the full afternoon *sea breeze* blows in.

Another consideration is wind direction. If the weather report predicts a strong, southerly *sea breeze* in the late afternoon you may want to start your sail earlier in the day and head toward the south. When the strong breeze fills in you will enjoy a comfortable *broad reach* home rather than slugging it out sailing *close-hauled* against strong winds and waves.

When sailing, keep your eyes open for threatening weather such as large thunder head clouds, squall lines, and small white fluffy clouds in front of a dark gray sky, or just a sudden blowing of sand on the beach. Different areas can have different warning signs, so ask your instructor or other sailors for common signs of bad weather and in what direction to look. Head to shore at the first sign of bad weather.

***

TIP *If you do bring your mobile phone on board (always in a waterproof bag and secured to you or the boat), you can get an update on the weather forecast and check the weather radar (especially important if thunderstorms are in the forecast).*

TIDE AND CURRENT

On certain parts of the planet, the tidal range between high and low tides can be as much as 40 feet. This movement of the water is caused by the gravitational force of the moon and sun pulling on the large bodies of water. Sailors should be aware if they are sailing in an area with large tidal ranges since it will affect the depth of the water and where they can sail.

↓ 10 KTS	↓ 10 KTS	↓ 10 KTS	Variable	8-10 KTS ↗	12 KTS ↗	15 KTS 🌧 ↗	18 KTS 🌧 ↗	17 KTS ↗
09.00	10.00	11.00	12.00	13.00	14.00	15.00	16.00	17.00

chance of thunderstorm

10am set sail for island on a broad reach

3pm boat all put away before big breeze and possible storm

1pm set sail for home on a broad reach

11.30 am beach the boat and have a picnic

Consider the weather forecast when planning your day's sail so you make the best use of the wind and avoid storms.

Current is the movement of water caused by any number of forces including tides, wind or river flow. Sailing on a *current* is like walking on a moving sidewalk. It can make you go faster or slower depending on whether you are sailing with or against the *current*. Use visual signs like "wakes" on buoys or anchored boats to assess *current* flow and determine the direction and speed of the *current*. New sailors should avoid sailing in strong *currents*.

In areas that are affected by *currents*, you will want to be wary of the direction of the *current* and how it may change during your sail. One of the more frustrating experiences for a sailor is to be caught "down *current*" in light winds, fighting against a strong *current* to get home.

GOING AGROUND

No sailor wants their boat or underwater fins to hit the bottom – and that's why you learn about the underwater topography of your sailing area from your instructor or a local sailor and by looking at a nautical chart. If you do happen to hit bottom in a small boat,

With *current* flowing parallel to both boats, their speed over the bottom will be affected. Boat A will be ripping out of the river fast, while boat B will be crawling in against the *current*.

BOAT A

CURRENT

BOAT B

WIND

it's usually pretty easy to get sailing again. You may be able to simply increase *heel* or pull up the *centerboard* (and *rudder*) a bit and sail right off into deep water. If the water is too shallow or the wind direction and situation don't allow an easy sail off – then you may have to get your feet wet and push. First, stop the boat by *heading up* and *luffing* the sails and then assess the best way to get back into deep water. You may want to lower your sails, and in extreme circumstances – wait for help. In tidal areas, know the time and heights of high and low water.

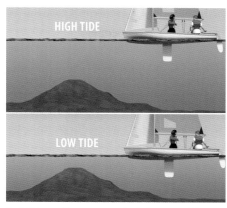

HIGH TIDE

LOW TIDE

Don't hit bottom! Pay attention to depth changes in tidal regions.

Out in the open ocean, the *current* flow is running perpendicular to the desired course of the two catamarans and will affect their course. Boat C doesn't take the *current* effect into account and points directly toward the destination. As they sail closer to the river mouth they are pushed farther downstream and have to change course radically. Boat D is smarter and adjusts their course to account for the sideways push of the *current*. Their path is straight into the river mouth – crabbing along in the sideways *current*.

③

②

①

BOAT C

BOAT D

③

②

①

CURRENT

SAILING IN A CONFINED AREA

You may sometimes launch in a crowded harbor where boats or shallow water prevent you from sailing off in any direction. First, take a moment to survey the situation. Consider the wind direction and plan the simplest and safest course to open water. Be especially wary of getting to a spot where you can't sail downwind because of some obstruction (shallow water, etc.) Plan a course that has some open water farther downwind. Then, if you have some problem, you have room to bear away or drift without hitting anything.

Another important consideration is boat speed. Similar to a bike or car, with speed comes maneuverability; so it is very important to keep moving in tight quarters. Avoid excessive *tacking* or sailing too close to the wind – because they both rob boat speed. When You Meet Other Boats In the United States, the USCG Navigation Rules and Regulations Handbook (available online) contains the many regulations governing boaters (from big ships to little dinghies) on inland and international waters. Amongst its pages are the rules covering

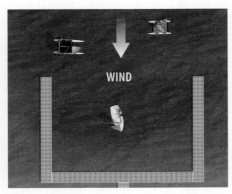

Beware of confined areas, especially if there is no open water downwind where you can drift if you have a problem. Stay upwind of the *"lee shore"*.

how boats should steer to avoid a possible collision. A fundamental rule is that all boats should keep a lookout. This means paying attention to all the boats near you – and watch for possible close encounters so that you don't find yourself in a situation trying to avoid a collision at the last minute. You may have to adjust course or look under the *mainsail* regularly to be aware of boats in the blind spot created by your sails.

TIP *Any time the wind is blowing toward the land – you must be aware of your proximity to that shore – since the land and the* no sail zone *can limit your maneuvering options.*

The navigation rules specify that when two boats approach each other, one is classified as the *give-way* boat. It must keep out of the way of the other boat by taking early and substantial action to keep well clear. The other boat, referred to as the *stand-on* boat, shall hold its course and speed unless it appears that the *give-way* boat is not taking appropriate action. Which boat is which depends on the type of boat and the situation.

Rule 18 states that a sailboat is the *stand-on* boat when approaching a power boat (which is the give-way boat). But there is an important exception: if the powerboat is restricted in its ability to maneuver (e.g., a big ship or yacht) or if it's *heading down* a narrow channel – then the sailboat must *give-way*.

TIP *Don't be a "sea lawyer" and push your stand-on status with a power boat – sail smart and if possible adjust your course far enough away that a "close call" with a power boat never develops.*

WIND

OVERTAKING BOAT GIVES WAY

Here are three basic rules governing sailboats approaching another sailboat.

■ For boats sailing on opposite *tacks*, the *starboard tack* boat is the *stand-on* boat and the *port tack* sailboat should give-way. (Usually it's best for the *port tack* boat to turn and steer behind the other boat).

■ For sailboats on the same *tack* the boat to *windward* should give-way to the leeward boat.

■ An overtaking boat must *give-way* to the boat being overtaken.

REMEMBER If you are the *give-way* boat, make your maneuver very obvious and early. Don't show off and cut things too close. Don't make the other boat guess your plan.

WIND

SAME TACK:
WINDWARD
GIVES WAY

OPPOSITE TACK:
PORT GIVES WAY

COMING HOME

Just like sailing in tight quarters, the key to bringing your sailboat back to land is wind direction and speed control. Always consider the wind direction and try to make your final approach sailing on a *close reach*. As you've learned, on this point of sail you can really control your speed (by easing the *mainsheet* and *luffing* the sail) without sacrificing maneuverability.

PRACTICE MAKES PERFECT

Do some practice trials in open water near a reference point such as a buoy. Practice steering the boat straight on a *close reach* as you let your sails out by easing *sheets*. Your speed will slowly drop, but at any time you can trim in the *sheets* again to accelerate. This technique will allow a slow-walking speed approach to the dock or mooring buoy. In stronger winds, you will have to allow for quite a bit of sideslip (*leeway*) downwind as your boat slows down. REMEMBER Don't get hurt – keep your hands inside the rail of the boat when landing against a dock.

Whenever possible, avoid landing your boat on a dock or beach that requires approaching on a *broad reach* or *run*. This type of landing (known as a downwind landing) is extremely hard on the boat and

WIND

If possible, approach the dock on a *close reach* so you can control your speed.

A tricky, downwind beach landing performed well.

can be quite dangerous because it is nearly impossible to effectively slow down and still maintain steering control. Do whatever you can to avoid a downwind landing, including asking people to move their boats to make space for you on the proper (leeward) side of the dock.

Sometimes a downwind landing is impossible to avoid. This is often the case when landing on a beach with the *sea breeze* blowing in. Unless the wind is perfectly perpendicular to the shore, you should approach on the *tack* that allows the "tightest" point of sail so you can try and *luff* the sails. As you get close, lift the *centerboard*, halfway (no more or the boat will not be able to head up to stop) so it will not hit the bottom. You can unclip the latch on the *rudders* if there is one and raise them halfway too. When you are close enough to shore to stand in the water turn the boat briskly toward the wind and have a crew

member (or bystander) jump in and grab the *bow* of the boat to keep it pointed into the wind while you prepare the boat for moving back to shore (e.g. lower sails, pull up the *centerboard*, remove *rudder* etc.). On a small catamaran, you could kick up the *rudders* and sail straight back onto the beach if it is sandy. But even in the best conditions – this will "scuff up" the bottom of your boat – and over time it could do some real damage. Better to take the landing step by step – slow and in control.

Don't get off the boat onto the dock or a beach until the sails are either fully *luffing* (or lowered) and someone is holding the boat by the *bow* (or it's tied up with its *bow line*). Practice these skills and learn how your boat reacts to different conditions so you can leave and return to a dock easily. If it looks like the docking will not go well, steer away and try again. In tight quarters it can be difficult to judge when to begin your slowing.

KNOTS AND ROPE

Knowing how to handle rope and making knots is a very important part of good seamanship (the art and skill of handling, working, and navigating any boat). Your instructor will explain how to tie these knots easily and quickly.

PRACTICE IS THE "KEY".

Two characteristics of a good knot are:
- ■ It holds well (does not come untied).
- ■ It is easy to untie even after heavy loading.

These six knots are used regularly by sailors:

BOWLINE

A great "loop" knot for tying *sheets* and *halyards* onto sails because once tight, it can take a great deal of shaking without untying. It is useful anytime a loop is needed.

ROUND TURN AND TWO HALF HITCHES

A good strong "attachment" knot that is very easy and fast to tie. It doesn't handle shaking very well – so a bowline is better for tying *sheets* to a sail.

CLEAT HITCH

A knot used primarily to secure the boat to a dock or a *halyard* to a fixed "T" shaped *cleat*.

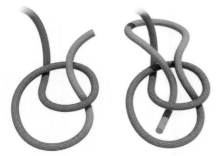

FIGURE EIGHT KNOT

A "stopper" knot tied at the very ends of *halyards* and *sheets* to prevent them from unintentionally running out through a *fairlead* or *block*.

SQUARE KNOT

A knot used to secure the two ends of a *line* together. Not secure when shaken.

CLOVE HITCH

Another "attachment" knot – doesn't like "shaking" and not as easy to untie as a Round Turn and Two Half Hitches.

THROWING A LINE

Another good sailing skill is to be able to throw a rope accurately and far. This comes in handy when trying to get a tow or in docking situations. Here's how:
1. Coil or flake the *line* well.
2. Put a few of the coils (about 10 feet) in your throwing hand.
3. Hold your "other" hand open, palm up, pointing at the target (so the coils on the hand can feed out.)
4. With your throwing hand – use a forceful underhand throw aiming slightly above the target.

REMEMBER Ropes on a sailboat are called *"lines"* – but they are the same thing.

SAIL CARE

Proper sail care will ensure long life for your sails. Different types of sails require different techniques to put them away after use. The bottom *line* is that you want a sail to remain as smooth and un-creased as possible. The best way to do this – especially for full battened catamaran sails is to roll it – from the top downwards. Sails without *battens* can be folded – from the bottom to the top accordion style and then put in a sail bag. Never stuff a sail or crumple it into a bag. And if the sail is going to be left in storage for any length of time – make sure the sail is dry.

FOLDED SAIL

ROLLED SAIL

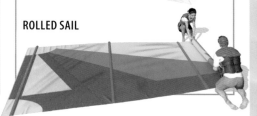

SAILING INTO THE FUTURE

Congratulations! You are now a sailor. Where you take your new-found sailing skills is now up to you. You should definitely spend some time building your experience, practicing and becoming a more skilled sailor.

With time on the water, your ability to handle the boat in stronger winds will improve – as will your "feel" of wind direction and the forces on the boat and sails. If possible, try sailing different boats – and gain some experience from the different perspectives of driver and crew.

From here – the world of sailing awaits. By learning to sail in a small boat you have a great foundation to build on no matter what direction you want to take your sailing. Maybe you want to try bigger boats. Small

keelboats require very similar skills to those you have mastered on the small boat. Their heavy fixed keel significantly reduces the risk of *capsize*, but they can carry lots of sail area and provide for a fun ride. Bigger keelboats have special equipment like winches to help you harness the higher loads involved.

You may get attracted to sailboat racing – or you may want to explore the world of cruising in a sailboat. There are so many possibilities, and so much more to learn as a new sailor. The American Sailing Association (ASA) can provide structure to your continuing education as a sailor. You may have picked up this book as part of an ASA110 sailing course. ASA's educational system can take you from here – at the beginning all the way to offshore passages – sailing across the ocean. For some of you, the next step in your education will be to take the ASA101 Basic Keelboat Sailing course. Others will want to keep sailing small boats, refining and honing their skills. There is no "right" path in the sport, just as there is no "right" type of boat – as long as you keep learning.

Wherever you decide to take your sailing – remember to "feel" the wind, stay safe and always have fun!

REVIEW QUESTIONS (see page 96 for answers)

CHOOSE FROM THE ANSWERS PROVIDED

1 Answer the following statements "True" or "False".

a The crew's side to side position in the boat is a very important way of controlling heel

b The rules for trimming a jib on a reach are different than for trimming a mainsail

c A good way to determine which jib sheet to trim is to see which side the jib will flap on if all sheets are released

d A centerboard is only necessary in strong winds

e Sailors in centerboard boats should be familiar with the shallow underwater topography (e.g. rocks and sandbars) that are shown on a nautical chart

f Sailors in centerboard boats do not care about the current because it does not affect them

g A rolled sail should have no wrinkles to help preserve the sail

2 When sailing in a confined area you should: (choose all the best answers)

a Sail as close as possible to any channel or shoal markers

b Keep a good lookout, especially in the blind spot behind the sails

c Keep your speed up because that is when the boat is most maneuverable

d Always be aware of the wind direction and the danger of too little open water to leeward of your course (lee shore)

e You don't have to worry about power boats because you have right of way

3 The best point of sail to approach a dock or buoy is: (choose all the best answers).

a Straight upwind

b A close reach because you have the best control over your speed on this point of sail

c A beam reach because all of your options are open

d A broad reach because that is the fastest point of sail

e With all sails lowered, slowly drifting toward the dock

4 Answer the following statements "True" or "False".

a When two boats sailing on opposite tacks approach each other – the port tack boat should "give way"

b When a sailboat under sail meets a large powerboat in a narrow, confining channel – the powerboat should give way

c If you are the "give way" vessel you should wait to the last minute to make your course change so you are sure of avoiding a collision

5 When planning to sail in an unfamiliar place you should consult the following sources of information. (Choose all that apply)

a Nautical chart showing the bottom contour, deep and shallow water

b A marine forecast for wind and waves

c The advice of experienced local sailors

d Look at the sky before you depart

6 What knot is best for attaching a jib sheet to the clew of the jib? (Choose the best answer)

a Square knot

b Bowline

c Round turn and two half hitches

d Cleat hitch

e Sheet bend

GLOSSARY

A

Abeam Direction (either left or right) away from the boat's *centerline* at an angle perpendicular to the boat's heading

Aft Direction toward the boat's *stern*

Ahead Direction in front of the boat parallel to the boat's heading

Astern Direction behind the boat directly opposite to the boat's heading

Asymmetrical See *Spinnaker*

Athwartships Across the boat in a sideways direction

B

Bailer A bucket or other device used to remove water from the *cockpit* or boat's interior

Batten Stiff slat inserted into a pocket in the sail to help control sail shape

Batten pocket The pocket on a sail that holds the *batten*

Beam reach Point of sail when the angle between the wind and the boat's course is about 90 degrees

Bearing away See *Heading down*

Beating See *Close-hauled*

Block Pulley used to lead ropes like *sheets* and *halyards* cleanly on the boat. Multiple *blocks* can be used together to provide mechanical advantage

Boom A horizontal pole supporting the bottom of the *mainsail*

Boom vang Sail trim system (usually made of *line* and *blocks)* running from *boom* to *mast* often used on windier *reaches* and *runs* to hold the *boom* down and create an efficient sail shape

Bow The boat's front end

Bow line rope tied at the bow of a boat that can be used for attaching to a dock, mooring or dolly

Broad reach Point of sail when the angle between the wind and the boat's course is about 100 – 170 degrees

By the lee Dangerous point of sail "past" a *run* when wind is coming over the same side of the boat as the *boom*

C

Cam cleat A common cleat employed on small boats that will hold *lines* – especially the *sheets*

Capsize Turning the boat over in the water – either on its side or all the way upside down

Centerboard The retractable, unballasted center fin on a dinghy or catamaran that rotates down into the water to keep the boat from side slipping (moving sideways) under sail

Centerline The imaginary line running from the *bow* to the *stern* in the middle of the boat

Chain plate Attachment point for standing rigging (such as *forestay* and *shrouds*) on the *hull*

Cleat A fitting used to secure ropes – there are many types of *cleats*

Clevis pin A metal pin used to secure a *shroud* or *forestay* to the boat

Clew Back lower corner of a sail

Close-hauled Point of sail when the angle between the wind and the boat's course is about 45 degrees. It is the closest point of sail to the wind

Close reach Point of sail when the angle between the wind and the boat's course is around 50 – 85 degrees

Cockpit The area inside of the *hull* of some boats where the crew puts their feet

Coming about Changing *tacks* by turning the *bow* of the boat through the wind

Cotter pin or cotter ring Light wire pin or loops used to secure a *clevis pin* in place

Cunningham See *Downhaul*

Current The movement of water caused by tides or wind

D

Daggerboard A *centerboard*-like fin that is raised and lowered vertically through a slot in the *hull*

Death roll An exciting way to *capsize* when the boat rolls over to *windward*

Downhaul Adjustable sail trim system rigged near a sail's *tack* and used to tension the *luff* of the sail

Drysuit Special sailing or diving suit with seals that keep a person totally dry even when swimming

F

Fairlead An eye or *block* used as a guide for *lines* (eg. *Jib* lead)

Feathering Heavy air steering technique used to reduce *heel* by steering slightly closer to the wind in order to spill power from the sails – also known as *pinching* when you do it in lighter winds

Fly a hull The act of sailing a catamaran with so much *heel* that the *windward hull* is out of the water flying through the air

Foot Bottom edge of sail

Forestay Standing rigging (usually wire)

that supports the *mast* – running from the *mast* to the *bow*

Foredeck The area between the *mast* and the *bow*

Forward Direction toward the *bow*

Foul weather gear Waterproof outer clothing worn by sailors to stay warmer and dry when sailing

G

Gennaker See *Asymmetrical*

Gooseneck Hinged attachment point for the *boom* on the *mast*

Groove Narrow band of steering for efficient *close-hauled* sailing – about 3 degrees wide

Gudgeon A small fitting at the *stern* used to attach the *rudder* to the *hull*, see *Pintle*

H

Halyard Rope or wire attached to the top of the sail and used to hoist it e.g. *main halyard* or *jib halyard*

Hank A metal, rope or cloth device used to secure the front of the *jib* to the *forestay*

Head Top corner of sail

Heading down Turning the boat away from the wind without changing *tacks* – also known as *bearing away*

Heading up Turning the boat toward the wind without changing *tacks* – also known as *luffing* up

Headstay See *Forestay*

Heel The tilting of the boat sideways caused by strong winds pushing on the sail

Hiking out The act of leaning out over the side of the boat to reduce *heel*

Hiking stick A *tiller* "extension" allowing for easier steering from a variety of positions

Hiking straps Foot straps used to lean out (hike out) over the side of the boat

Hull The boat's outer body. The *hull* of a boat floats on the water

I

In irons Predicament when the boat is "stuck" pointed directly toward the wind – in the *no sail zone* – with sails flapping and the boat not moving through the water

J

Jib A sail used in addition to a *mainsail* that sits in front of the *mast*, normally it is tacked to the *bow*

Jib halyard *Halyard* for the *jib*

Jibe To turn the boat so that its *stern* passes through the wind

Jibing Changing *tacks* by turning the boat away from the wind

Jib sheet Rope(s) attached to the *clew* of the *jib* used to control the "trim" of the *jib*

K

Keelboat Sailboat that has a heavy lead or iron keels that cannot be moved like a *centerboard*. Usually seen on larger (over 20 feet) boats

L

Leech Back edge of sail

Lee shore Downwind shore that your boat would blow toward if you stopped sailing

Leeward Direction away from the wind or the downwind side of an object

Life jacket Flotation vest or similar device worn by small boat sailors for safety

Line Any piece of rope on a sailboat

Luff Front edge of sail

Luffing The shaking of a sail like a flag when the *sheet* is released

M

Main halyard *Halyard* for the *mainsail*, see *Halyard*

Mainsail The primary, *aft*-most sail on a boat with one *mast*. Normally the *luff* is attached to the *mast*

Mainsheet Rope used to control the adjustment or "trim" of the *mainsail* – the sail's primary trim control

Mast The vertical pole that supports the sails

Mast step Fitting upon which the *mast* stands

N

No sail zone An area about 90 degrees wide – bisected by the wind direction – inside of which a sailboat cannot sail because the sails will not fill

O

Outhaul Adjustable sail control system that attaches to the *mainsail*'s *clew* and is used to tension the sail's *foot*

P

PFD Personal Flotation Device, see *Life Jacket*

Pinching See *Feathering*

Pintle A pin-type device used to attach a *rudder* to the *hull*, see *gudgeon*

Planing Sailing along super-fast, skimming along over the water on a *reach* or a *run*

Points of sail Words used to describe the angle between the wind and the sailboat's course

Port Left

Port tack Sailing with the wind coming over the boat's left side

Q

Quick tow A good way to bailout a swamped *"swamper"* with a powerboat tow

R

Reach All *points of sail* between a *run* and *close-hauled*

Righting line A *line* secured underneath the *trampoline* of a catamaran to facilitate righting the boat when *capsized*

Ring ding See *Cotter pin*

Rudder A movable steering fin at the back of the *hull*

Run Point of sail when the wind is directly behind the boat

S

Sea breeze Common fair weather, summertime wind on big lakes and oceans. It blows toward the land

Sculling To rapidly flap the *rudder* by pushing and pulling the *tiller* to propel the boat

Shackle U-shaped metal (or rope) device used to fasten sails and fittings to other parts of the boat

Sheet Rope used to control the trim of a sail (eg., *mainsheet, jib sheet*). *Sheets* are the primary sail trim control

Shroud A wire or fiber *line* running from the side of the *hull* to a point up the *mast* that helps to support the *mast*

Spinnaker A large lightweight sail set in front of the *mast* used for faster sailing on *reaches* and downwind

Spreader A strut attached to the *mast* and one of the side *shrouds* designed to help support the *mast*

Starboard Right

Starboard tack Sailing with the wind coming over the boat's right side

Stern The boat's back end

Swamper A boat that has no flotation tanks and requires outside assistance to rescue after a *capsize*

T

T-cleat A common *cleat* used on small boats to secure *halyards*

Tack (1) The bottom front corner of a sail

Tack (2) The act of *tacking*

Tack (3) The side of the boat the wind is on (*port tack* or *starboard tack*)

Tacking See *coming about*

Telltales Yarn, sailcloth or ribbon used to show wind direction and wind flow. Often tied to a *shroud* or taped to the *luff* of a sail

Tiller The steering arm that connects to and moves the *rudder(s)*

Tiller arm The steering arm that attaches to the front of each *tiller* on a catamaran

Tiller crossbar See *Tiller arm*

Trampoline The material secured between a catamaran's two *hulls* that facilitates crew movement

Transom The boat's back end

Traveler Adjustable system upon which the *mainsheet* or its *block(s)* can slide across the boat – a sail trim device

Turn turtle The position of the *capsized* boat when the *mast* is pointed straight down

W

Whitecaps Waves with white frothy tops that are formed in winds over 12 knots

Windward Direction toward the wind – or the upwind side of an object

Winging the jib Holding the *jib* out to catch wind on the *windward* side of the boat. This can only be performed when sailing on a *run* with the wind straight behind

INDEX

Bold entries show illustrations or diagrams.

ANSWERS TO REVIEW QUESTIONS

BEGINNING TO SAIL
page 24 answers

1 d
2 a, c, d, e
3 a
4 b, e
5 d
6 a
7 b
8 False
9 d

LET'S GO SAILING
page 52 answers

1 d
2 b, c
3 a False
  b True
  c False
  d False
  e False
  f False
4 a
5 d
6 a, c, d
7 b, c, d

SAFE SAILING
page 68 answers

1 a False
  b True
  c False
  d False
  e False
  f False
  g False
2 a, b, e
3 c
4 a False
  b False
  c False
  d True
5 d
6 b
7 a False
  b False
  c False
  d True
  e True

SKILLS AND CONCEPTS FOR EVERY SAILOR
page 88 answers

1 a True
  b False
  c True
  d False
  e True
  f False
  g True
2 b, c, d
3 b
4 a True
  b False
  c False
5 a, b, c, d
6 b

ACKNOWLEDGEMENTS

ASA is deeply grateful to the following people: Jeff Riecks ASA instructor; Hobie Cat Company; Jerry Garcia; Bebe; Chris Wright and the Mission Bay Yacht Club; Billy Black and Rob Migliaccio.

Photography credits
ASA would like to thank the following for their kind permission to reproduce their images: Bitter End Yacht Club/John Glynn: Front cover, p7; Hobie Cat Company: p34, p43, p71, p87; Billy Black: Back cover, p6, p26, p49, p54, p63, p66; Peter Isler: p27; Rob Migliaccio: p5, p28, p30, p47, p50, p55, p67, p70